Study Guide
IT4IT™
Foundation

The Open Group Publications available from Van Haren Publishing

The TOGAF Series:
TOGAF® Version 9.1
TOGAF® Version 9.1 – A Pocket Guide
TOGAF® 9 Foundation Study Guide, 3rd Edition
TOGAF® 9 Certified Study Guide, 3rd Edition

The Open Group Series:
The IT4IT™ Reference Architecture, Version 2.1
IT4IT™ for Managing the Business of IT – A Management Guide
IT4IT™ Foundation Study Guide, 2nd edition
The IT4IT™ Reference Architecture, Version 2.1 – A Pocket Guide
Cloud Computing for Business – The Open Group Guide
ArchiMate® 3.0 – A Pocket Guide
ArchiMate® 2 Certification – Study Guide
ArchiMate® 3.0 Specification

The Open Group Security Series:
O-TTPS - A Management Guide
Open Information Security Management Maturity Model (O-ISM3)
Open Enterprise Security Architecture (O-ESA)
Risk Management – The Open Group Guide
The Open FAIR™ Body of Knowledge – A Pocket Guide

All titles are available to purchase from:
www.opengroup.org
www.vanharen.net
and also many international and online distributors.

Study Guide
IT4IT™ Foundation

Preparation for the IT4IT Part 1 Examination
2nd Edition

Prepared by Andrew Josey & Michelle Supper

Colophon

Title:	IT4IT™ Foundation Study Guide, Second edition
Series:	The Open Group Series
A Publication of:	The Open Group
Authors:	Andrew Josey and Michelle Supper
Publisher:	Van Haren Publishing, Zaltbommel, www.vanharen.net
ISBN Hardcopy:	978 94 018 0193 5
ISBN eBook:	978 94 018 0194 2
ISBN: ePub	978 94 018 0195 9
Edition:	Second edition, first impression, July 2017
Layout and Cover Design:	Coco Bookmedia, Amersfoort – NL
Copyright:	© 2017, The Open Group All rights reserved

No part of this publication may be reproduced, stored in a retrieval system, or transmitted, in any form or by any means, electronic, mechanical, photocopying, recording, or otherwise, without the prior permission of the copyright owner.

The views expressed in this Study Guide are not necessarily those of any particular member of The Open Group.

In the event of any discrepancy between text in this document and the official IT4IT documentation, the IT4IT documentation remains the authoritative version for certification, testing by examination, and other purposes. The official IT4IT documentation can be obtained online at www.opengroup.org/it4it

Study Guide
IT4IT™ Foundation: Preparation for the IT4IT Part 1 Examination, 2nd Edition
Document Number: B177

Published by The Open Group, May 2017.

Comments relating to the material contained in this document may be submitted to:

The Open Group, Apex Plaza, Forbury Road, Reading, Berkshire, RG1 1AX, United Kingdom
or by electronic mail to: ogspecs@opengroup.org

Contents

Chapter 1 Introduction 1
1.1 Key Learning Points 1
1.2 The Open Group IT4IT Certification Program 1
    1.2.1 Program Vision and Principles 2
    1.2.2 Certification Document Structure 2
    1.2.3 IT4IT Foundation 3
    1.2.4 IT4IT Foundation Certification Syllabus Overview 3
    1.2.5 The Certification Process 4
    1.2.6 Preparing for the Examination 8
1.3 Summary 8
1.4 Recommended Reading 8
1.5 Exercises 9
1.6 Test Yourself Questions 9

Chapter 2 IT4IT Overview 11
2.1 Key Learning Points 11
2.2 An Introduction to the IT4IT Reference Architecture 11
2.3 The IT Value Chain 12
2.4 Summary 18
2.5 Recommended Reading 19
2.6 Exercise 1: IT4IT Overview 19
2.7 Test Yourself Questions 20

Chapter 3 Key Terminology 21
3.1 Key Learning Points 21
3.2 Key Terms 21
    3.2.1 Service Lifecycle Data Object 21
    3.2.2 IT Value Chain 22
    3.2.3 Value Chain 22
    3.2.4 Value Stream 22
    3.2.5 Functional Component 22
    3.2.6 Service Model Backbone Data Object 23
    3.2.7 Relationship 23
    3.2.8 System of Record 23
    3.2.9 IT Service 23
    3.2.10 Configuration Item (CI) 24

3.3	Summary	24
3.4	Recommended Reading	24
3.5	Exercise 2: Definitions	24
3.6	Test Yourself Questions	25

Chapter 4 Basic Concepts ... 27

4.1	Key Learning Points	27
4.2	The Strategy to Portfolio (S2P) Value Stream	27
4.3	The Requirement to Deploy (R2D) Value Stream	29
4.4	The Request to Fulfill (R2F) Value Stream	31
4.5	The Detect to Correct (D2C) Value Stream	34
4.6	The IT4IT Reference Architecture	36
	4.6.1 The Service Model	37
	4.6.2 The IT4IT Information Model	38
	4.6.3 The IT4IT Functional Model	40
	4.6.4 Functional Components	41
	4.6.5 Functional Components and Data Objects	41
	4.6.6 The IT4IT Integration Model	42
	4.6.7 IT Service	43
4.7	Summary	43
4.8	Recommended Reading	44
4.9	Exercise 3: Basic Concepts	44
4.10	Test Yourself Questions	45

Chapter 5 IT4IT Core ... 47

5.1	Key Learning Points	47
5.2	IT4IT Abstractions	47
5.3	Level 1 Concepts	49
	5.3.1 Value Streams	51
	5.3.2 Functional Components	51
	5.3.3 Service Lifecycle Data Objects	52
	5.3.4 Relationships	52
	5.3.5 Level 1 Reference Architecture Model	53
5.4	Level 2 Concepts	55
	5.4.1 Level 2 Reference Architecture Diagram (Example)	56
5.5	Level 3 Concepts	56
5.6	Levels 4 and 5	58
5.7	Summary	60

5.8	Recommended Reading	60
5.9	Exercise 4: IT4IT Core	60
5.10	Test Yourself Questions	62

Chapter 6 The Strategy to Portfolio Value Stream 65

6.1	Key Learning Points	65
6.2	Objectives	65
6.3	Benefits	66
6.4	Key Performance Indicators	67
6.5	Functional Components	68
	6.5.1 Enterprise Architecture Functional Component	69
	6.5.2 Policy Functional Component	69
	6.5.3 Proposal Functional Component	70
	6.5.4 Portfolio Demand Functional Component	70
	6.5.5 Service Portfolio Functional Component	71
	6.5.6 IT Investment Portfolio Auxiliary Functional Component	72
6.6	Summary	72
6.7	Recommended Reading	73
6.8	Exercise 5: Strategy to Portfolio Value Stream	73
6.9	Test Yourself Questions	74

Chapter 7 The Requirement to Deploy Value Stream 77

7.1	Key Learning Points	77
7.2	Objectives	77
7.3	Benefits	78
7.4	Key Performance Indicators	78
7.5	Functional Components	80
	7.5.1 Project Functional Component	81
	7.5.2 Requirement Functional Component	82
	7.5.3 Service Design Functional Component	82
	7.5.4 Source Control Functional Component	83
	7.5.5 Build Functional Component	84
	7.5.6 Build Package Functional Component	85
	7.5.7 Release Composition Functional Component	86
	7.5.8 Test Functional Component	87
	7.5.9 Defect Functional Component	87
7.6	Summary	88
7.7	Recommended Reading	88

7.8	Exercise 6: Requirement to Deploy Value Stream	88
7.9	Test Yourself Questions	90

Chapter 8 The Request to Fulfill Value Stream ... 93

8.1	Key Learning Points	93
8.2	Objectives	93
8.3	Benefits	94
8.4	Key Performance Indicators	94
8.5	Functional Components	95
	8.5.1 Engagement Experience Portal Secondary Functional Component	97
	8.5.2 Offer Consumption Functional Component	99
	8.5.3 Offer Management Functional Component	100
	8.5.4 Catalog Composition Functional Component	100
	8.5.5 Request Rationalization Functional Component	101
	8.5.6 Fulfillment Execution Functional Component	102
	8.5.7 Usage Functional Component	103
	8.5.8 Chargeback/Showback Functional Component	103
	8.5.9 Knowledge & Collaboration Supporting Function	104
8.6	Summary	104
8.7	Recommended Reading	105
8.8	Exercise 7: Request to Fulfill Value Stream	105
8.9	Test Yourself Questions	107

Chapter 9 The Detect to Correct Value Stream ... 109

9.1	Key Learning Points	109
9.2	Objectives	109
9.3	Benefits	109
9.4	Key Performance Indicators	111
9.5	Functional Components	112
	9.5.1 Service Monitoring Functional Component	113
	9.5.2 Event Functional Component	114
	9.5.3 Incident Functional Component	114
	9.5.4 Problem Functional Component	115
	9.5.5 Change Control Functional Component	116
	9.5.6 Configuration Management Functional Component	116
	9.5.7 Diagnostics & Remediation Functional Component	117
	9.5.8 Service Level Functional Component	117

9.6	Other IT Operations Areas	118
9.7	Summary	119
9.8	Recommended Reading	119
9.9	Exercise 8: Detect to Correct Value Stream	119
9.10	Test Yourself Questions	121

Appendix A Answers to Exercises and Test Yourself Questions   123

A.1	Answers to Exercises	123
	A.1.1 Exercise 1: IT4IT Overview	123
	A.1.2 Exercise 2: Definitions	124
	A.1.3 Exercise 3: Basic Concepts	125
	A.1.4 Exercise 4: IT4IT Core	127
	A.1.5 Exercise 5: Strategy to Portfolio Value Stream	129
	A.1.6 Exercise 6: Requirement to Deploy Value Stream	131
	A.1.7 Exercise 7: Requirement to Fulfill Value Stream	133
	A.1.8 Exercise 8: Detect to Correct Value Stream	135
A.2	Answers to the Test Yourself Questions	138

Appendix B Test Yourself Examination Paper   143

| B.1 | Examination Paper | 143 |
| B.2 | Questions | 143 |

Appendix C Test Yourself Examination Paper Answers   153

| C.1 | Scoring the Examination | 153 |
| C.2 | Answers | 153 |

Appendix D Functional Component & Data Object Summary   159

| D.1 | Functional Components | 159 |
| D.2 | Data Objects | 163 |

Appendix E IT4IT Foundation Certification Syllabus   167

Acronyms and Abbreviations   175

Index   177

Preface

This Document

This book is a Study Guide for IT4IT™ Foundation. It is based on The Open Group Certification for People: IT4IT™ Conformance Requirements (Level 1). It gives an overview of every learning objective for the IT4IT Foundation certification syllabus and in-depth coverage on preparing and taking the IT4IT Part 1 Examination. It is specifically designed to help individuals to prepare for certification. This 2nd Edition of the document has been updated to align with the IT4IT Reference Architecture, Version 2.1.

The Open Group Certification for People: IT4IT Certification Program is intended to make certification available to people who have knowledge and understanding of the IT4IT Reference Architecture.

The IT4IT Reference Architecture presents the IT service lifecycle in a new and powerful way, and provides a foundation on which to base your IT operating model. Adoption of the Reference Architecture can accelerate IT's transition to becoming a service broker to the business. It can also address the strategic challenges brought about by the implementation of mobility, cloud, big data, security, and Bring Your Own Device (BYOD).

The use of the IT4IT approach allows organizations to:
- Focus on the true role of IT: to deliver services that make the company more competitive and innovative
- Support the multi-sourced service economy, enabling new experiences in driving the self-sourcing of services to power innovation

The audience for this Study Guide includes:
- Individuals who require a basic understanding of the IT4IT Reference Architecture
- IT Professionals/Practitioners who are responsible for delivering services in a way that is flexible, traceable, and cost-effective
- IT Professionals who want to achieve a higher-level certification in the IT4IT Certification Program (when available) in a stepwise approach

A prior knowledge of IT Service Management is advantageous but not required. While reading this Study Guide, the reader should also refer to the IT4IT documentation available at www.opengroup.org/it4it.

The Study Guide is structured as follows:
- Chapter 1 (Introduction) provides a brief introduction to The Open Group IT4IT Certification Program, specifically the IT4IT Foundation certification, and explains how to use this Study Guide as well as how to prepare for the examination
- Chapter 2 (IT4IT Overview) provides a first introduction to the IT4IT Reference Architecture, the IT Value Chain, and the four value streams that make up with IT Value Chain
- Chapter 3 (Key Terminology) describes the terminology of the IT4IT Reference Architecture
- Chapter 4 (Basic Concepts) describes the scope, value propositions, and typical activities of the four value streams, as well as the basic concepts of the IT4IT Reference Architecture, including the Service Model, the Information Model, and the Functional Model
- Chapter 5 (IT4IT Core) describes the five abstraction levels of the IT4IT Reference Architecture and the key concepts of each level
- Chapter 6 (The Strategy to Portfolio Value Stream) describes the objectives, benefits, Key Performance Indicators (KPIs), functional components, and data objects of the Strategy to Portfolio Value Stream
- Chapter 7 (The Requirement to Deploy Value Stream) describes the objectives, benefits KPIs, functional components, and data objects of the Requirement to Deploy Value Stream
- Chapter 8 (The Request to Fulfill Value Stream) describes the objectives, benefits, KPIs, functional components, and data objects of the Request to Fulfill Value Stream
- Chapter 9 (The Detect to Correct Value Stream) describes the objectives, benefits, KPIs, functional components, and data objects of the Detect to Correct Value Stream
- Appendix A (Answers to Exercises and Test Yourself Questions) provides the answers to the Exercises and Test Yourself sections provided at the end of each chapter
- Appendix B (Test Yourself Examination Paper) provides a Test Yourself examination to allow you to assess your knowledge of the

IT4IT Reference Architecture and readiness to take the IT4IT Part 1 Examination
- Appendix C (Test Yourself Examination Paper Answers) provides the answers to the examination in Appendix B
- Appendix D (Functional Component & Data Object Summary) provides summary tables of the IT4IT Reference Architecture functional components and data objects
- Appendix E (IT4IT Foundation Certification Syllabus) provides the IT4IT Foundation certification syllabus

How to Use this Study Guide
The chapters in this Study Guide are arranged to provide coverage of the IT4IT Foundation certification syllabus (see Appendix E) and should be read in order. However, you may wish to use this Study Guide during review of topics with which you are already familiar, and it is certainly possible to select topics for review in any order. Where a topic requires further information from a later part in the syllabus, a cross-reference is provided.

Each chapter includes:
- "Key Learning Points" and "Summary" sections to help you to easily identify what you need to know for each topic
- A "Recommended Reading" section that indicates the relevant sections in the IT4IT Reference Architecture that can be read to obtain a further understanding of the subject material
- "Exercises" and "Test Yourself Questions" sections that will help you to check your understanding of the chapter, and prepare for the IT4IT Part 1 Examination; these include open questions, simple exercises, and multiple-choice format questions where you must identify one correct answer

Finally, at the end of this Study Guide is a "Test Yourself" practice examination paper that you can use to test your readiness to take the official IT4IT Part 1 Examination.

Conventions Used in this Study Guide
The following conventions are used throughout this Study Guide in order to help identify important information and avoid confusion over the intended meaning.

- Ellipsis (…)
  Indicates a continuation; such as an incomplete list of example items, or a continuation from preceding text.
- **Bold**
  Used to highlight specific terms.
- *Italics*
  Used for emphasis. May also refer to other external documents.
- *(Syllabus Reference: Unit X, Unit Name, Learning Outcome Y: Statement)*
  Used at the start of a text block to identify the IT4IT Foundation certification syllabus learning outcome. For example, *Syllabus Reference: Unit 2, Definitions, Learning Outcome 1* refers to the first learning outcome in Unit 2. If a learning outcome has subsidiary outcomes then a notation Y-N is used; e.g., 1-1, 1-2.

In addition to typographical conventions, the following conventions are used to highlight segments of text:

A Note Box is used to highlight useful or interesting information.

A Tip Box is used to provide key information that can save you time or that may not be entirely obvious.

About The Open Group

The Open Group is a global consortium that enables the achievement of business objectives through IT standards. With more than 500 member organizations, The Open Group has a diverse membership that spans all sectors of the IT community – customers, systems and solutions suppliers, tool vendors, integrators, and consultants, as well as academics and researchers – to:

- Capture, understand, and address current and emerging requirements, and establish policies and share best practices

- Facilitate interoperability, develop consensus, and evolve and integrate specifications and open source technologies
- Operate the industry's premier certification service

Further information on The Open Group is available at www.opengroup.org.

The Open Group publishes a wide range of technical documentation, most of which is focused on development of Open Group Standards and Guides, but which also includes white papers, technical studies, certification and testing documentation, and business titles. Full details and a catalog are available at www.opengroup.org/bookstore.

Readers should note that updates – in the form of Corrigenda – may apply to any publication. This information is published at www.opengroup.org/corrigenda.

About the Authors

Andrew Josey, The Open Group

Andrew Josey is VP Standards and Certification, overseeing all certification and testing programs of The Open Group. He also manages the standards process for The Open Group. Since joining the company in 1996, Andrew has been closely involved with the standards development, certification, and testing activities of The Open Group. He has led many standards development projects including specification and certification development for the ArchiMate®, TOGAF®, POSIX®, and UNIX® programs.

He is a member of the IEEE, USENIX, UKUUG, and the Association of Enterprise Architects (AEA). He holds an MSc in Computer Science from University College London.

Michelle Supper, Science Inspired Ltd.

Following a PhD in X-ray astrophysics, Michelle started participation in The Open Group, and turned her analytical skills to architecture. Specializing in remedial architectures in MoDAF and the TOGAF® standard, she is often relied upon to resolve tricky problems, and rescue stalled projects. She has served as system architect for three major defense programs, and as a consultant Enterprise Architect for several multi-million pound projects in the UK Home Office, Ministry of Justice, and UK Ministry of Defence. Now an independent consultant and Managing Director of her own company, she can be found at www.scienceinspired.com.

Trademarks

ArchiMate®, DirecNet®, Making Standards Work®, OpenPegasus®, The Open Group®, TOGAF®, UNIX®, UNIXWARE®, X/Open®, and the Open Brand X® logo are registered trademarks and Boundaryless Information Flow™, Build with Integrity Buy with Confidence™, Dependability Through Assuredness™, EMMM™, FACE™, the FACE™ logo, IT4IT™, the IT4IT™ logo, O-DEF™, O-PAS™, Open FAIR™, Open Platform 3.0™, Open Process Automation™, Open Trusted Technology Provider™, Platform 3.0™, SOSA™, the Open O™ logo, and The Open Group Certification logo (Open O and check™) are trademarks of The Open Group.

COBIT® is a registered trademark of the Information Systems Audit and Control Association (ISACA) and the IT Governance Institute.

eTOM® is a registered trademark of the TM Forum.

ITIL® is a registered trademark of AXELOS Ltd.

OMG®, Unified Modeling Language®, and UML®, are registered trademarks of the Object Management Group, Inc. in the United States and/or other countries.

All other brand, company, and product names are used for identification purposes only and may be trademarks that are the sole property of their respective owners.

Acknowledgements

The Open Group gratefully acknowledges:
- Past and present members of The Open Group IT4IT Forum for developing the IT4IT Reference Architecture
- The following reviewers of this Study Guide:
    - Corinne Brouch
    - Sukumar Daniel
    - Steve Else
    - Ohad Goldfarb
    - Martin Kirk
    - Sylvain Marie
    - Ed Roberts
    - Pavel Sekanina
    - Bart Verbrugge

References

The following documents are referenced in this Study Guide:
- ArchiMate® 3.0 Specification, Open Group Standard, C162, June 2016, published by The Open Group; refer to: www.opengroup.org/bookstore/catalog/c162.htm
- M. Porter: Competitive Advantage: Creating and Sustaining Superior Performance, ISBN: 978-0684841465, Free Press; 1st Edition (June 1998)
- The Open Group IT4IT™ Reference Architecture, Version 2.1, Open Group Standard, C171, January 2017, published by The Open Group; refer to: www.opengroup.org/bookstore/catalog/c171.htm
- The Open Group IT4IT™ Reference Architecture, Version 2.1 Reference Cards, N170, January 2017, published by The Open Group; refer to: www.opengroup.org/bookstore/catalog/n170.htm
- The Open Group® Certification for People: IT4IT™ Conformance Requirements, Version 1.1, X1702, April 2017, published by The Open Group; refer to: www.opengroup.org/bookstore/catalog/x1702.htm
- Unified Modeling Language (UML), Object Management Group (OMG); refer to: www.uml.org

The following web links are referenced in this Study Guide:
- The Open Group IT4IT Certification website: www.opengroup.org/certifications/it4it

Chapter 1
Introduction

1.1 Key Learning Points

This document is a Study Guide to The Open Group Certification for People: IT4IT Certification Program.

It covers every learning objective of the IT4IT Foundation certification syllabus, and has learning resources that have been specifically designed to prepare individuals who wish to take and pass the IT4IT Part 1 Examination.

This first chapter will familiarize you with The Open Group IT4IT Certification Program and its principles, and also provide important information about the structure of the examination.

The objectives of this chapter are as follows:
- To provide an understanding of IT4IT certification and why you should become certified
- To learn key facts about the IT4IT Part 1 Examination

1.2 The Open Group IT4IT Certification Program

(Syllabus Reference: Unit 9, IT4IT Certification Program, Learning Outcome 1: You should be able to explain The Open Group IT4IT Certification Program and distinguish between the levels for certification.)

Certification is available to individuals who wish to demonstrate that they have attained the required knowledge and understanding of the IT4IT Reference Architecture.

At the time of writing there is a single level defined for IT4IT certification:
- Level 1: IT4IT Foundation

1.2.1 Program Vision and Principles

The vision for the program is to define and promote a market-driven education and certification program to support the IT4IT Reference Architecture. The program has been designed with the following principles in mind:

Table 1: Certification Principles

Principle	Certification Aspects
Openness	The program is open to applicants from all countries.
Fairness	Certification is achieved only by passing an examination that is equivalent to that taken by any other candidate.
Market Relevance	The program is structured to meet the perceived needs of the market.
Learning Support	Training courses are provided by third parties.
Quality	Training course providers may choose to seek Open Group accreditation for their courses. Accredited courses are listed on The Open Group website. Only accredited courses may use The Open Group logo.
Best Practice	The program is designed to follow industry best practice for equivalent certification programs.

1.2.2 Certification Document Structure

The documents available to support the program are as shown in Figure 1.

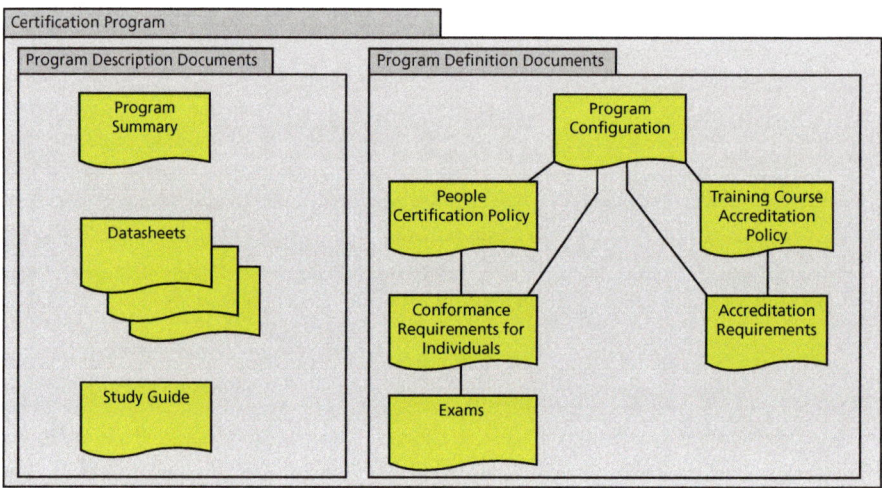

Figure 1: Certification Document Structure

Program description documents, such as this Study Guide, are intended for an end-user audience including those interested in becoming certified. The program definition documents are intended for trainers, examination developers, and the Certification Authority. All of these documents are available from The Open Group website.[1]

> **Why become Certified?**
> Becoming certified demonstrates publicly that you understand the IT4IT Reference Architecture. The Open Group publishes the definitive directory of IT4IT certified individuals and issues certificates.

1.2.3 IT4IT Foundation

The purpose of certification for IT4IT Foundation is to provide validation that the candidate has gained knowledge of the fundamentals of the IT4IT Reference Architecture, including knowledge of the terminology, structure, and basic concepts. The learning objectives at this level focus on knowledge and comprehension. Certification for IT4IT Foundation is achieved by passing the IT4IT Part 1 Examination; this is a multiple-choice examination with 40 questions.[2]

1.2.4 IT4IT Foundation Certification Syllabus Overview

Individuals holding the IT4IT Foundation certification will have demonstrated their understanding of:
- The basic concepts of the IT4IT Reference Architecture and the IT Value Chain
- The concepts of IT4IT Core
- The key terminology of IT4IT
- The four value streams:
  - The Strategy to Portfolio Value Stream
  - The Requirement to Deploy Value Stream
  - The Request to Fulfill Value Stream
  - The Detect to Correct Value Stream
- The IT4IT Certification Program

---

1. Available from the IT4IT certification website at: www.opengroup.org/certifications/it4it or from The Open Group Bookstore at www.opengroup.org/bookstore.
2. For the latest information on examinations, see the IT4IT certification website at: www.opengroup.org/certifications/it4it.

1.2.5 The Certification Process

This Study Guide is aimed at preparing you to become certified for IT4IT Foundation. An overview of the certification process is shown in Figure 2 (using ArchiMate® notation).

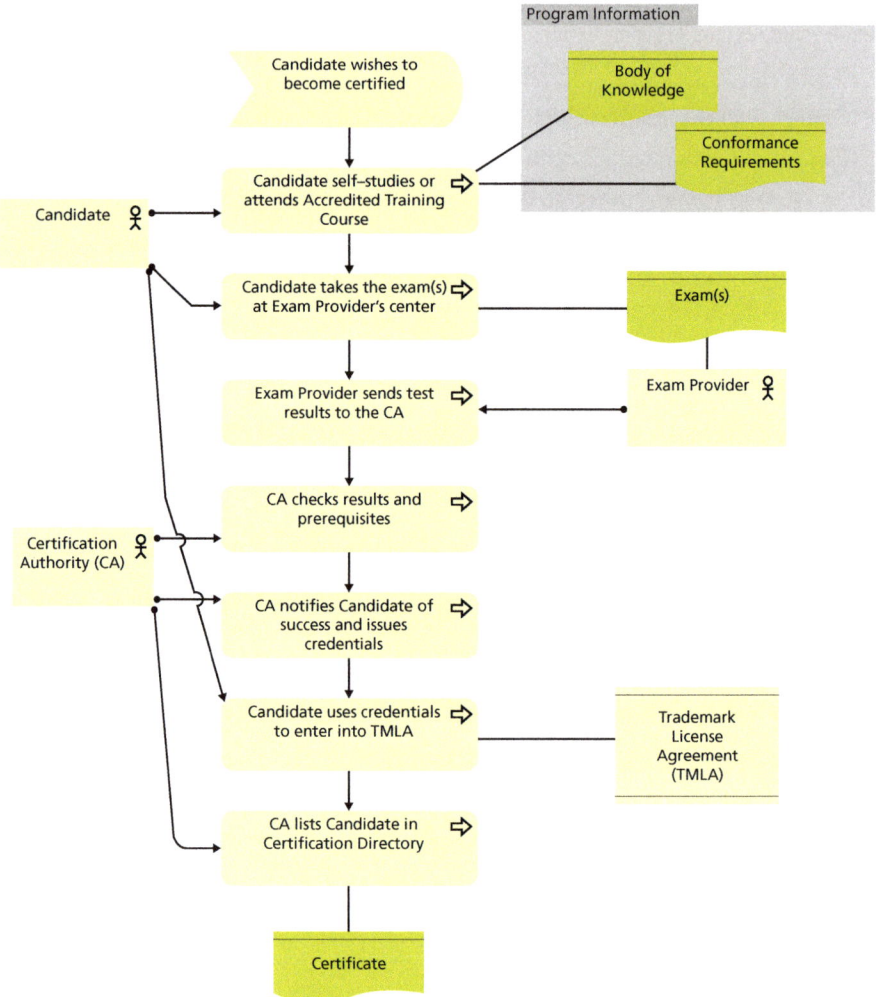

Figure 2: Certification Process

The process for becoming certified as shown in Figure 2 is as follows:

1. Candidate wishes to become certified.

    To achieve IT4IT Foundation certification, the candidate must possess a thorough knowledge and understanding of those elements of the IT4IT

Reference Architecture identified in the Conformance Requirements as being mandatory.

2. Candidate self-studies or attends an Accredited Training Course.

   A candidate can self-study or attend an Accredited Training Course. The two key inputs to the learning process are the IT4IT Reference Architecture itself and the Conformance Requirements. The Conformance Requirements identify which elements of the IT4IT Reference Architecture must be known to achieve certification.

3. Candidate takes the examination(s) at Examination Provider's test center.

   Certification is achieved by passing the applicable examination(s) delivered at The Open Group Examination Provider's test center. Candidates who fail to meet the required pass mark will be informed of this and are encouraged to undergo further study and re-sit the examination at a later date. Candidates who fail an examination are not allowed to re-sit an examination again for a period as defined in the current retake policy for the program, which is available from the Certification Authority's website. At of the time of writing this period is one (1) month.

4. Certification Authority (CA) checks results and prerequisites.

   The examination results of all Candidates will be sent to the Certification Authority for review. The Certification Authority will ensure that the pass mark has been achieved, and also check that Candidates have not failed an examination within the previous month.

5. Certification Authority notifies candidate of success and issues credentials.

   The Certification Authority will notify the candidate in writing of their decision. If the application for certification is accepted, the Certification Authority will issue credentials that will enable the successful candidate to access the Certification Authority's website to accept the terms of, and enter into, a Trademark License Agreement (TMLA) with the Certification Authority.

6. Candidate uses credentials to enter into Trademark License Agreement. The candidate can then use the credentials to access the Certification Authority's website to enter into a TMLA with the Certification Authority and to obtain the artwork of the applicable Program Logo.

7. Certification Authority lists candidate in Certification Directory.

The Certification Authority will then make a Certificate available to the candidate in electronic form, and enter the candidate's Certification Record into the Certification Directory. The credentials will also allow the Certified Person to control to whom the Certification Record is disclosed and to update their contact and employer information in the Certification Record.

1.2.5.1 IT4IT Part 1 Examination Coverage by Topic

The IT4IT Foundation certification syllabus can be found in Appendix E. The topic areas are weighted; those with higher weighting are considered to be more important, and this is reflected in the examination. The topic areas covered by the examination together with the number of questions per area in the examination are provided in Table 2. It should be noted that Unit 9 is non-examinable.

Table 2: IT4IT Part 1 Examination Coverage

Unit	Topic	No. of Questions
1	IT4IT Overview	4
2	Definitions	0
3	Basic Concepts	8
4	IT4IT Core	8
5	Strategy to Portfolio Value Stream	5
6	Requirement to Deploy Value Stream	5
7	Request to Fulfill Value Stream	5
8	Detect to Correct Value Stream	5
9	The Open Group IT4IT Certification Program	0

Format of the examination questions

The examination comprises multiple-choice questions that are very similar in format to the Test Yourself practice examinations included in Appendix B. Note that the exact format for display is test center-specific, and will be made clear on the screens when taking the examination.

> **Tips when Taking the Examination**
>
> Ensure you take the on-screen tutorial provided prior to the commencement of the examination. This will explain how the examination will work and will not use any of the allotted time for the examination. Please read each question carefully before considering the answer options. Be aware that while some questions may seem to have more than one right answer, you are to look for the one that makes the most sense and is the most correct. If you are unsure of an answer, mark the question and come back to it later if you have time. Attempt to answer all questions, as leaving questions unanswered will reduce your maximum possible score.

What do I need to bring with me to take the examination?

You should consult with the test center prior to attendance regarding the forms of picture ID you will be required to bring with you to verify your identification.

Can I refer to materials while I take the examination?

No, the IT4IT Part 1 Examination is closed book.

What is the pass mark?

You should check with The Open Group for the latest information on the examination. At the time of writing the pass mark for the examination is 65%.

If I fail, how soon can I retake the examination?

You should consult the current policy on The Open Group website. At the time of writing, the policy states that individuals who have failed the examination are not allowed to retake the examination within one (1) month.

1.2.6 Preparing for the Examination

You can prepare for the examination by working through this Study Guide. A mapping of the sections of this Study Guide to the IT4IT Foundation certification syllabus is given in Appendix D. After completing each section, you should read the referenced parts from the IT4IT Reference Architecture together with any other recommended reading, and then complete the Test Yourself Questions.

Once you have completed all the sections in this Study Guide, you can then attempt the Test Yourself practice examination paper in Appendix B. This has been designed to thoroughly test your knowledge. If you have completed your studies and can attain a pass mark for the Test Yourself examination paper, then it is likely you are ready to sit the examination.

1.3 Summary

The Open Group IT4IT Certification Program is a knowledge-based certification program. Currently it has one level: IT4IT Foundation.

This Study Guide will prepare you for IT4IT Foundation.

To prepare for the examination:
- Work through this Study Guide step-by-step
- At the end of each chapter, read the sections of the IT4IT Reference Architecture and other references listed under Recommended Reading, and complete the Exercises and the Test Yourself Questions
- Once you have completed all the chapters in this Study Guide, attempt the Test Yourself practice examination paper given in Appendix B
- If you can attain the target score for the Test Yourself practice examination paper, then you have completed your preparation, and you should be ready to take the IT4IT Foundation examination

1.4 Recommended Reading

The following are recommended sources of further information for this chapter:

- The Open Group® Certification for People: IT4IT™ Conformance Requirements, Version 1.1, X1702, April 2017, published by The Open Group; refer to: www.opengroup.org/bookstore/catalog/x1702.htm
- The Open Group IT4IT Certification Program website: www.opengroup.org/certifications/it4it

1.5 Exercises

There are no exercises for this chapter.

1.6 Test Yourself Questions

Q1: Which one of the following describes three principles of The Open Group IT4IT Certification Program?
   A. Integrity, Scalability, Flexibility
   B. Objectivity, Robustness, Simplicity
   C. Openness, Fairness, Quality
   D. Knowledge-based, Valuable, Simplicity

Q2: Which of the following topic areas is *non-examinable* in the IT4IT Foundation certification syllabus?
   A. IT4IT Overview
   B. Basic Concepts
   C. Strategy to Portfolio Value Stream
   D. The Open Group IT4IT Certification Program

Q3: Which of the following statements about the retake policy for IT4IT examinations is correct?
   A. Candidates who fail cannot take an examination again within one (1) month.
   B. Candidates who fail cannot take an examination again within five (5) days.
   C. Candidates who fail cannot take an examination again within seven (7) days.
   D. Candidates who fail cannot take an examination again within three (3) months.

Chapter 2

IT4IT Overview

2.1 Key Learning Points

This chapter will help you understand the IT4IT Reference Architecture.

Key Points Explained
This chapter will help you to:
- Gain a first introduction to the IT4IT Reference Architecture
- Understand the IT Value Chain
- Understand how the IT Value Chain and value streams support the IT service lifecycle
- Obtain a brief overview of the four value streams that make up the IT Value Chain

2.2 An Introduction to the IT4IT Reference Architecture

(Syllabus Reference: Unit 1, IT4IT Overview, Learning Outcome 1: You should be able to explain what The Open Group IT4IT Reference Architecture is and what approach it uses.)

The Open Group IT4IT Reference Architecture is a standard reference architecture for managing the business of IT. It uses a value chain approach to model the functions that IT performs, in order to help organizations identify the activities that contribute to business competitiveness.

(Syllabus Reference: Unit 1, IT4IT Overview, Learning Outcome 2: You should be able to identify the intended use of IT4IT Reference Architecture for organizations.)

The IT4IT Reference Architecture provides a "standard, repeatable model" for creating an IT management ecosystem. It is intended to help organizations adapt to changes in technology, process, and methods without having to re-factor the management architecture to accommodate every shift.

(Syllabus Reference: Unit 1, IT4IT Overview, Learning Outcome 3: You should be able to identify the intended use of the IT4IT Reference Architecture for suppliers of IT management products and services.)

The IT4IT Reference Architecture is intended to function as design guidance for suppliers of IT management products and services.

(Syllabus Reference: Unit 1, IT4IT Overview, Learning Outcome 4: You should be able to list the guiding principles that the IT4IT framework adheres to.)

The guiding principles for the IT4IT framework are that it should be:
- Flexible enough to support frequent changes in business models while sturdy enough to track compliance and cost controls
- Defined in practical terms for immediate application in "real-world" IT environments
- Able to be implemented in a phased approach that avoids any requirement for rip and replace
- Technology and vendor-agnostic
- Accessible to anyone who wishes to make use of it
- Wherever possible, complementary to current industry standard best practices

2.3 The IT Value Chain

(Syllabus Reference: Unit 1, IT4IT Overview, Learning Outcome 5: You should be able to demonstrate understanding of the IT Value Chain.)

A value chain is a sequence of activities performed by an organization in order to deliver something valuable, such as a product or service. As the product or service passes through each of the activities, it gains some value. A value chain framework helps organizations to identify the activities that are especially important for competitiveness, such as those which advance strategy and achieve goals.

Figure 3 shows the IT Value Chain. It shows the series of activities that IT performs to add value to a service. The value chain approach provides a model familiar to executives, and shows how the architectural components are all related. The Service Backbone is shown in the center of the diagram and ties the value streams together and ties the value streams to the supporting activities.

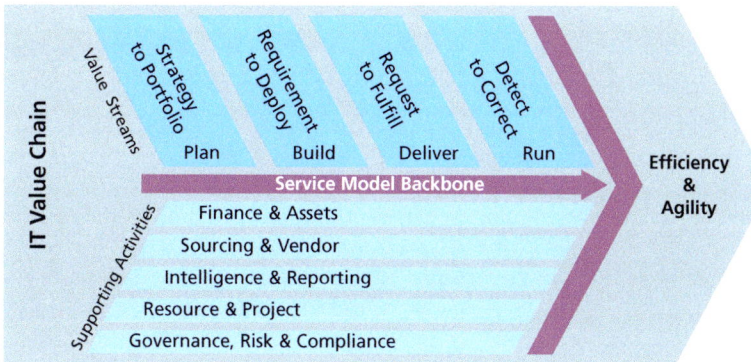

Figure 3: IT Value Chain

(Syllabus Reference: Unit 1, IT4IT Overview, Learning Outcome 6: You should be able to briefly describe the difference between the primary activities and supporting activities in the IT Value Chain.)

The IT Value Chain is grouped into two main categories of activities:
- Primary activities, which are concerned with the production of goods or the delivery of services for which a business function, like IT, is directly accountable; this includes activities such as planning, production, consumption, fulfillment, and support
- Supporting activities, which facilitate the efficiency and effectiveness of the primary activities; examples of supporting activities include management; these are activities that are shared across the whole enterprise and are not IT-specific

(Syllabus Reference: Unit 1, IT4IT Overview, Learning Outcome 7: You should be able to list the primary activities of the IT Value Chain.)

The primary activities of the IT Value Chain are known as value streams and are:
- Strategy to Portfolio
- Requirement to Deploy
- Request to Fulfill
- Detect to Correct

These primary activities have a vital role in helping to run the full service lifecycle holistically.

(Syllabus Reference: Unit 1, IT4IT Overview, Learning Outcome 8: You should be able to list the supporting activities of the IT Value Chain.)

The supporting activities for the IT Value Chain are:
- Finance & Assets
- Sourcing & Vendor
- Intelligence & Reporting
- Resource & Project
- Governance Risk & Compliance

The supporting activities help ensure the efficiency and effectiveness of the IT Value Chain and primary value streams. These can be corporate or administrative functions that are hosted in the lines of business and/or IT.

(Syllabus Reference: Unit 1, IT4IT Overview, Learning Outcome 9: You should be able to explain the difference between a value chain and a value stream.)

The value streams are the ordered activities within the value chain; in the case of the IT Value Chain shown in Figure 3 they can be characterized as Plan, Build, Deliver, and Run. Each value stream is concerned with a key aspect of the service model, together with the essential data objects (Information Model), and functional components (Functional Model) that support it.

(Syllabus Reference: Unit 1, IT4IT Overview, Learning Outcome 10: You should be able to briefly describe how the IT Value Chain supports the IT service lifecycle.)

The IT Value Chain describes the IT service lifecycle. The IT service lifecycle is described by the IT Value Chain, together with the four value streams (see Section 3.2.4).

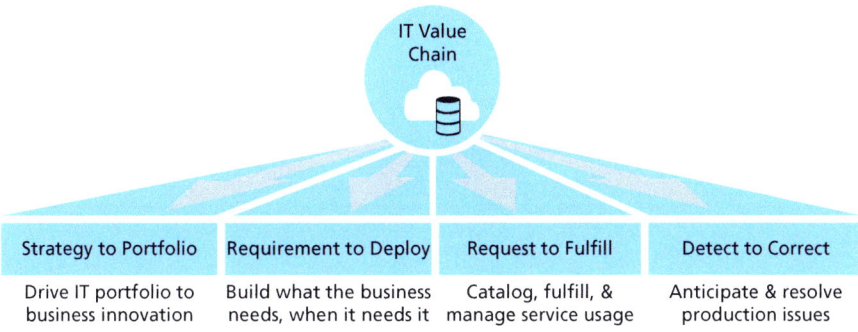

Figure 4: Value Streams Overview

(Syllabus Reference: Unit 1, IT4IT Overview, Learning Outcome 11: You should be able to briefly describe how the four value streams manage the full service lifecycle.)

Each value stream encapsulates capabilities that are necessary to manage aspects of the service lifecycle. These capabilities are realized as a set of functional components (see Section 3.2.5) and data objects (see Section 3.2.1). The functional components within the four value streams are responsible for creating, refining, and tracking key data objects across the full service lifecycle. The relationships between the data objects that pass between the four value streams during the service lifecycle are well defined.

Functional Components and Data Objects

(Syllabus Reference: Unit 3, Basic Concepts, Learning Outcome 5: You should be able to describe what functional components and data objects are.)

Functional components are the smallest technology unit that can stand alone and be useful as a whole to a customer.

Data objects represent tangible, non-trivial data items that are owned, consumed, produced, or modified by the functional components.

(Syllabus Reference: Unit 3, Basic Concepts, Learning Outcome 6: You should be able to explain the relationship of functional components to data objects.)

Functional components must have defined input(s) and output(s) that are data objects and it must change or advance a key data object (e.g., state change). Auxiliary functional components are not dedicated to a single value stream and provide relevant data objects to key functional components. Typically, functional components control a single data object.

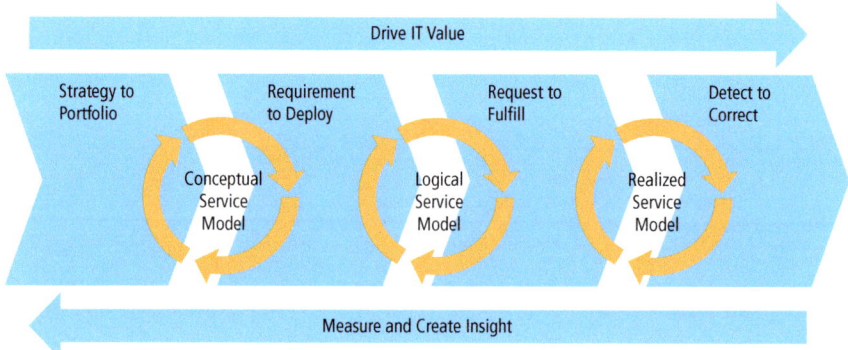

Figure 5: Value Streams and Service Models

The service lifecycle comprises:
1. The Conceptual Service Model, which describes why we need a service, who the customers are, how much it might cost, and what benefits might be realized through the implementation of the service.
2. The Logical Service Model, which provides a view of the service in terms of the components and capabilities that are needed to operate it.
3. The Realized Service Model, where a service is released and available in a Service Catalog for Subscription.

(Syllabus Reference: Unit 3, Basic Concepts, Learning Outcome 1: You should be able to briefly describe an overview of the Strategy to Portfolio (S2P) Value Stream.)

The **Strategy to Portfolio (S2P) Value Stream** is the "plan" part of the "plan, build, deliver, run" of the IT Value Chain. This activity defines a strategy to balance and broker the IT portfolio: it drives the IT portfolio towards business innovation.

The S2P Value Stream receives strategic demands for new or improved services from the business or IT itself and develops a key data object, known as the Conceptual Service, to represent the new or enhanced service that is requested. The Conceptual Service is the bridge between business and IT in that it provides the business context for the service along with its high-level architectural attributes.

(Syllabus Reference: Unit 3, Basic Concepts, Learning Outcome 2: You should be able to briefly describe an overview of the Requirement to Deploy (R2D) Value Stream.)

The **Requirement to Deploy (R2D) Value Stream** is the "build" part of the "plan, build, deliver, run" of the IT Value Chain. This activity prioritizes every requirement to build the best services and deploy them: it builds what the business needs when it needs it.

The R2D Value Stream receives the Conceptual Service data object and uses it as a foundation to design and develop the Logical Service. The development takes into account detailed requirements that describe how the newly requested service and its components shall be designed. The Logical Service can be thought of as the name for the "service system" that is being created or enhanced, and which delivers the value to the business.

The Logical Service and designs lead to the creation of a Service Release, which is described in a Service Release Blueprint that describes how the service is instantiated and delivered.

The R2D Value Stream sources (builds, buys, or rents), tests, and delivers the deployable service (the Service Release Blueprint) to the R2F Value Stream.

(Syllabus Reference: Unit 3, Basic Concepts, Learning Outcome 3: You should be able to briefly describe an overview of the Request to Fulfill (R2F) Value Stream.)

The **Request to Fulfill (R2F) Value Stream** is the "deliver" part of the "plan, build, deliver, run" of the IT Value Chain. This activity handles each request for services through a streamlined process to fulfill it: it catalogs, fulfills, and manages service usage.

The R2F Value Stream receives the Service Release Blueprint and creates Service Catalog Entries which represent how the service is technically delivered. Service owners build out Offers based on the technical capabilities (Service Catalog Entries) that are available. The Offers are viewable to the consumer and can be ordered for a set price and service contract as detailed in the Offer. Once ordered, the R2F Value Stream is responsible for the tasks to transition the service into production, where the D2C Value Stream takes over the operational activities of the service.

(*Syllabus Reference: Unit 3, Basic Concepts, Learning Outcome 4: You should be able to briefly describe an overview of the Detect to Correct (D2C) Value Stream.*)

The **Detect to Correct (D2C) Value Stream** is the "run" part of the "plan, build, deliver, run" of the IT Value Chain. This activity seeks to detect issues and correct them before impacting users: it anticipates and resolves production issues.

The D2C Value Stream provides a framework to integrate the monitoring, management, remediation, and other operational aspects associated with realized services and/or those under construction. It also provides a comprehensive overview of the business of IT operations and the services these teams deliver. Output from the D2C Value Stream enters the lifecycle as new demands within the S2P Value Stream.

2.4 Summary

This chapter has introduced the IT4IT Reference Architecture.

The Open Group IT4IT Reference Architecture is a standard reference architecture for managing the business of IT. It uses a value chain approach to model the functions that IT performs in order to help organizations identify the activities that contribute to business competitiveness.

The IT Value Chain is a classification scheme for activities that add net value to products or services provided by or through the IT function. It includes primary activities such as planning, production, consumption, fulfillment, and support. It also includes supporting activities such as finance, human resource, governance, and supplier management.

Co-ordination of the IT Value Chain and its associated value streams is all made possible by the Reference Architecture that ties them all together.

2.5 Recommended Reading

The following are recommended sources of further information for this chapter:
- The IT4IT Reference Architecture, Version 2.1, Chapters 1 and 3

2.6 Exercise 1: IT4IT Overview

In your own words, provide short answers to these questions.

1. What is the IT4IT Reference Architecture and what approach does it use?

2. How should the IT4IT Reference Architecture be used by organizations?

3. What is the difference between primary activities and supporting activities in the IT Value Chain?

4. What are the primary activities of the IT Value Chain?

5. What is the difference between a value chain and a value stream?

6. How do the four value streams manage the full service lifecycle?

7. What is the Strategy to Portfolio Value Stream?

8. What is the Requirement to Deploy Value Stream?

9. What is the Request to Fulfill Value Stream?

10. What is the Detect to Correct Value Stream?

_____

_____

2.7 Test Yourself Questions

Q1: Which of the following describes the IT4IT Reference Architecture?
  A. A modeling language for describing Agile solutions
  B. An Enterprise Architecture framework
  C. A process-driven framework for IT Service Management
  D. A standard for managing the business of IT

Q2: Which of the following is a guiding principle for the IT4IT Reference Architecture?
  A. It is limited to concepts that suffice for modeling 80% of practical cases.
  B. It is flexible enough to support changes in business models.
  C. It is quantitative and can be used as the basis for metrics.
  D. It encapsulates all IT operations areas.

Q3: Which of the following describes the IT Value Chain?
  A. A series of activities that IT performs to add value to a business service
  B. A best practice framework focused on IT processes and capabilities
  C. A notation for specifying and documenting the IT Reference Architecture
  D. A schedule of IT projects for implementing a transition to an IT services model

Q4: Which of the following is considered to be a primary activity in the IT Value Chain?
  A. Finance
  B. Human Resources
  C. Planning
  D. Supplier Management

Chapter 3
Key Terminology

3.1 Key Learning Points

This chapter will help you understand the key terminology of the IT4IT Reference Architecture standard.

Key Points Explained
This chapter will help you to answer the following question:
- What are the key terms for IT4IT Foundation?

> The key terms listed and defined here are used in the rest of this Study Guide. The IT4IT Foundation syllabus expects candidates to understand and be able to explain the definitions marked as learning outcomes in this chapter.
> Please refer to this chapter when you need more information on the meaning of key terms used in other parts of this Study Guide.

3.2 Key Terms

(Syllabus Reference: Unit 2, Definitions, Learning Outcomes 1-9: You should understand and be able to explain the following definitions.)

3.2.1 Service Lifecycle Data Object

(Syllabus Reference: Unit 2, Definitions, Learning Outcome 1)

Data or records produced and/or consumed to advance or control the service model as it progresses through its lifecycle phases. Data objects can take a physical or digital form and are produced, consumed, or modified by functional components. Within the IT4IT Reference Architecture there are two classifications of data objects:
- Key data objects – those that are essential to managing or advancing the service lifecycle
- Auxiliary data objects – those that are important but not essential to the service lifecycle

3.2.2 IT Value Chain
(Syllabus Reference: Unit 2, Definitions, Learning Outcome 2)

A classification scheme for the set of primary and supporting activities which contribute to the overall lifecycle that creates net value for products or services provided by or through the IT function. Within the IT4IT framework, the IT Value Chain describes the model of the IT business function. It includes primary activities such as planning, production, consumption, fulfillment, and support. It also includes supporting activities such as finance, human resource, governance, and supplier management.

3.2.3 Value Chain
(Syllabus Reference: Unit 2, Definitions, Learning Outcome 3)

A classification scheme for the complete set of primary and supporting activities that contribute to the lifecycle that creates net value for a market offering.

Note: The value chain concept is derived from Michael Porter's book Competitive Advantage.

3.2.4 Value Stream
(Syllabus Reference: Unit 2, Definitions, Learning Outcome 4)

Describes the key activities for a discrete area within the IT Value Chain where some unit of net value is created or added to the service as it progresses through its lifecycle. The IT4IT framework describes four value streams (Strategy to Portfolio, Requirement to Deploy, Request to Fulfill, and Detect to Correct).

3.2.5 Functional Component
(Syllabus Reference: Unit 2, Definitions, Learning Outcome 5)

A software building block. The smallest unit of technology in the IT4IT Reference Architecture that can stand on its own and be useful as a whole to an IT practitioner (or IT service provider). Functional components they must have defined inputs and outputs that are data objects and they must have an impact on a key data object.

3.2.6 Service Model Backbone Data Object
(Syllabus Reference: Unit 2, Definitions, Learning Outcome 6)

Key data objects that annotate an aspect of the service model in its conceptual, logical, consumable, or physical state. Service Model Backbone data objects and their relationships form the Service Model Backbone which provides a holistic view of a service.

3.2.7 Relationship
(Syllabus Reference: Unit 2, Definitions, Learning Outcome 7)

Primarily used to depict the connections between (or interactions with) data objects. In the IT4IT Reference Architecture, relationships are based on three design principles:
- System of record – used to describe the relationships which control authoritative source data via a system-to-system interface. These relationships are prescriptive, in that they must be maintained to ensure the integrity of the IT4IT Reference Architecture.
- System of engagement – used to describe the relationships between data objects and humans or functional components via a user experience interface.
- System of insight – used to describe the relationships between data objects for the purpose of generating knowledge, information, or analytics.

3.2.8 System of Record
(Syllabus Reference: Unit 2, Definitions, Learning Outcome 8)

A synonym for a system that contains and/or controls authoritative source data.

Note: This term can be easily confused with system of record relationships.

3.2.9 IT Service
(Syllabus Reference: Unit 2, Definitions, Learning Outcome 9)

A performance of an act that applies computing and information management competencies or resources for the benefit of another party.

3.2.10 Configuration Item (CI)

A CI is defined as any component that may need to be managed in order to deliver an IT service.

3.3 Summary

This chapter lists and defines the key terms used in this Study Guide and the IT4IT Foundation syllabus. In most cases, these terms are used as part of the learning outcomes within other chapters of this Study Guide.

3.4 Recommended Reading

The following are recommended sources of further information for this chapter:

- The IT4IT Reference Architecture, Version 2.1, Chapter 2

3.5 Exercise 2: Definitions

1. Complete the first column in the following table, by entering the relevant number(s) to identify the definition matching the term.

Answer	Term	Definition
	Key Data Object	1. Those that are important but not essential to the service lifecycle.
	System of Insight	2. Primarily used to depict the connections between data objects.
	Auxiliary Data Object	3. Used to describe relationships between data objects for the purpose of generating knowledge, information, or analytics.
	Functional Component	4. Those essential to managing or advancing the service lifecycle.
	Relationship	5. The smallest unit of technology in the IT4IT Reference Architecture that can stand on its own, and be useful as a whole to an IT service provider.

3.6 Test Yourself Questions

Q1: Which classification of data object denotes those that are essential to managing the service lifecycle?
 A. Auxiliary
 B. Functional
 C. Key
 D. Secondary

Q2: Complete the sentence: The design principle used to describe relationships between data objects and functional components via a user experience interface is known as _____.
 A. System of engagement
 B. System of experience
 C. System of insight
 D. System of record

Q3: What is a functional component?
 A. A key activity for a value stream within the IT Value Chain
 B. A primary activity within the IT Value Chain that creates net value
 C. A record produced to advance the service model as it advances through the lifecycle
 D. A software building block

Q4: Complete the sentence: The _____ consists of key data objects that annotate aspects of the _____.
 A. auxiliary data object, Reference Architecture
 B. service lifecycle, Service Model
 C. Service Model Backbone, Service Model
 D. system of record, authoritative source data

Chapter 4
Basic Concepts

4.1 Key Learning Points

This chapter will help you understand the basic concepts of the value streams and the IT4IT Reference Architecture.

Key Points Explained

This chapter introduces the following:
- The scope, value propositions, and typical activities of the four value streams
- The basic concepts of the IT4IT Reference Architecture, including the Service Model, the Information Model, and the Functional Model
- Functional components
- The concept of the IT service

4.2 The Strategy to Portfolio (S2P) Value Stream

(Syllabus Reference: Unit 3, Basic Concepts, Learning Outcome 7: You should be able to describe the scope of the S2P Value Stream.)

The Strategy to Portfolio (S2P) Value Stream provides IT organizations with a framework to interconnect the different functions and activities involved in managing the portfolio of services delivered to the enterprise. These include capturing demand for IT services, prioritizing and forecasting investments, Service Portfolio Management, and Project Management.

Traditional IT planning and Portfolio Management activities emphasize capturing and tracking a collection of *projects* that represent the "orders" from the business for technology enablement. The S2P Value Stream places emphasis on the *service* delivered, and aims to provide a more holistic view of the IT portfolio. This improves data consistency and transparency, and helps to shape business investment decisions and maintain alignment between the business strategy and the IT portfolio by connecting IT costs with business value.

(Syllabus Reference: Unit 3, Basic Concepts, Learning Outcome 8: You should be able to list the S2P value propositions.)

The key value propositions for adopting the S2P Value Stream are as follows:
- Establish a holistic IT portfolio view across the IT PMO, the Enterprise Architecture functional component, and the Service Portfolio functional component, so that IT portfolio decisions are based on business priorities
- Use well-defined system of records between the key areas that contribute to the IT Portfolio Management function, in order to support consistent data and provide accurate visibility into business and IT demand
- Endorse a Service Model that provides full service lifecycle tracking through conceptual, logical, and physical domains, so it is possible to trace whether that which was requested was actually delivered

(Syllabus Reference: Unit 3, Basic Concepts, Learning Outcome 9: You should be able to list the S2P typical activities.)

There are four typical activities in the S2P Value Stream:

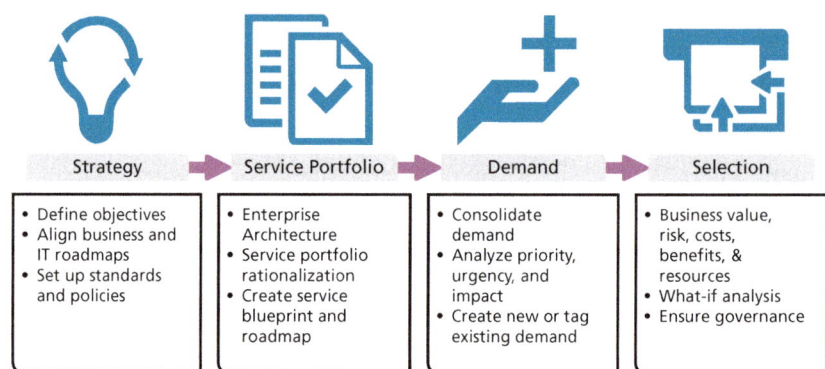

Figure 6: Strategy to Portfolio Activities

Strategy
This activity is about aligning IT strategy to the business strategy; specifically, aligning the business objectives and goals with the IT roadmaps. This ensures that investments are optimized to come out when the business needs them, and also prevents the unnecessary duplication of investments. IT strategies are created and documented, and the means by which they will be achieved is spelled out here.

Service Portfolio

This is about understanding the service portfolio and how it relates to the collection of assets. It is about ensuring that risk is managed, and that the investments in the portfolio will meet the business needs and IT objectives. Modeling the relationship between services and the business architecture is a key aspect of making investment decisions.

Demand

Demand comes from many different sources: change requests and enhancements, investment initiatives, major policy decisions, production side problems, patches, security issues, etc. The IT function will itself have a set of technology transformation changes that it has to track. This backlog has to be consolidated and prioritized.

Selection

This activity is focused on deciding which demands to address at any given point in time. There are often too many demands in the backlog to address, so there is a need to discriminate between them. The backlog has to be evaluated against a number of factors, including opportunity, cost, the amount of risk that the organization is willing to take on, the availability of scarce resources, etc. Given all of this, IT has to make a choice and the items that rise to the top become proposals.

4.3 The Requirement to Deploy (R2D) Value Stream

(Syllabus Reference: Unit 3, Basic Concepts, Learning Outcome 10: You should be able to describe the scope of the R2D Value Stream.)

The Requirement to Deploy (R2D) Value Stream provides the framework for creating/sourcing new services or modifying those that already exist. The goal of the R2D Value Stream is to ensure predictable, cost-effective, high quality results. It promotes high levels of re-use and the flexibility to support multi-sourcing. The R2D Value Stream is process-agnostic in that, while methods and processes may change, the functional components and data objects that comprise the value stream remain constant. Therefore, it is complementary to both traditional and new methods of service development like Agile, SCRUM, or DevOps.

The R2D Value Stream consumes the Conceptual Service produced in the S2P Value Stream. Through a series of design, development, or sourcing and testing functions, this enables the development of the Logical Service. The Logical Service is elaborated upon until it represents a release that can be commissioned into a production state using standard deployment methods or in an on-demand manner using a user-driven catalog experience. Once deployed into a production state, the Physical Service Model, comprising the physical elements that make up the service, will be generated.

(Syllabus Reference: Unit 3, Basic Concepts, Learning Outcome 11: You should be able to list the R2D value propositions.)

The key value propositions for adopting the R2D Value Stream are to:
- Ensure that the Service Release meets the business expectations (quality, utility)
- Make service delivery predictable, even across globally dispersed teams and suppliers, with multiple development methodologies, while preserving innovation
- Standardize service development and delivery to the point where re-use of service components is the norm
- Build a culture of collaboration between IT operations and development to improve Service Release success

(Syllabus Reference: Unit 3, Basic Concepts, Learning Outcome 12: You should be able to list the R2D typical activities.)

There are four typical activities in the R2D Value Stream:

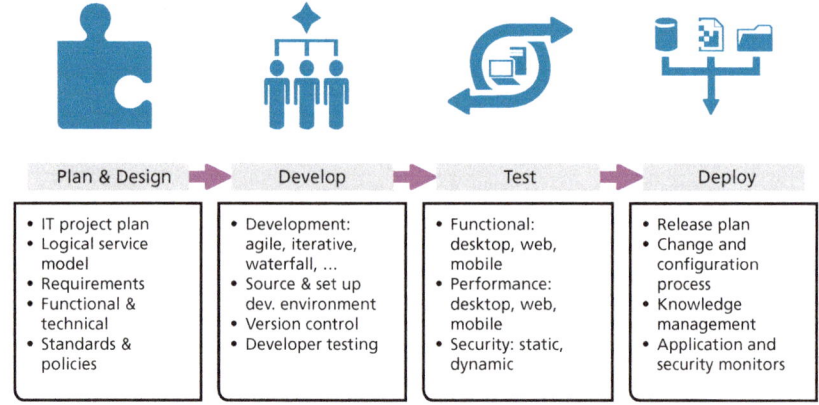

Figure 7: Requirement to Deploy Activities

The R2D Value Stream is a continuous development activity, not a one-time activity or a sequential activity and the activities are intertwined. An Agile methodology project might have all four activities happening every week.

Plan & Design
This activity involves planning and creating a detailed logical view of the service. It starts with the Scope Agreement that comes from the S2P Value Stream, and creates an initiative to manage the overall work. Logical design is then built upon the conceptual design, incorporating the functional and technical requirements as well as IT standards and policies.

Develop
Development, be it integration, sourcing services, or writing code, happens in all methodologies whether its waterfall, iterative, Agile, or others. This development is packaged depending on the specific components with the service. This activity also includes developer testing and unit testing.

Test
This is focused on three main areas:
1. Is the service functional from all user viewpoints (e.g., desktop, web, and mobile)?
2. Is the service meeting its performance criteria across multiple usage levels and devices?
3. Is the service secure? This can be checked by inspecting the code and probing the running service.

Deploy
Deployment starts with the release plan, which documents the parts and versions that come together to create the service. The plan needs to address how to integrate the service into the IT change and management configuration processes, how to troubleshoot the service, and how to monitor the availability, security, and performance aspects of the running service.

4.4 The Request to Fulfill (R2F) Value Stream

(Syllabus Reference: Unit 3, Basic Concepts, Learning Outcome 13: You should be able to describe the scope of the R2F Value Stream.)

The Request to Fulfill (R2F) Value Stream is a framework connecting the various consumers (business users, IT practitioners, or end customers) with goods and services that are used to satisfy productivity and innovation needs. The R2F Value Stream emphasizes time-to-value, repeatability, and consistency for consumers looking to request and obtain services from IT.

The R2F Value Stream helps IT to optimize both service consumption and fulfillment experiences for users by delineating functions for an Offer Catalog and Catalog Composition. The R2F Value Stream framework provides a single consumption experience to consumers for seamless subscription to both internal and external services. It also manages Subscriptions and routing fulfillments to different service providers.

The R2F Value Stream plays an important role in helping IT organizations transition to a service broker model. Enterprise customers have been using external suppliers for goods and services for many years. The IT multi-sourcing environment will accelerate as companies adopt cloud computing offerings like Infrastructure as a Service (IaaS), Platform as a Service (PaaS), and Software as a Service (SaaS).

(Syllabus Reference: Unit 3, Basic Concepts, Learning Outcome 14: You should be able to list the R2F value propositions.)

The key value propositions for adopting the R2F Value Stream are to:
- Provide a portal and catalog blueprint for facilitating a service consumption experience that allows consumers to easily find and subscribe to services through self-service, regardless of sourcing approach
- Establish the model for moving from traditional IT request management to service brokerage
- Increase fulfillment efficiency through standard change deployment and automation
- Leverage the common Service Model to reduce custom service request fulfillments and design automated fulfillments
- Facilitate a holistic view and traceability across service Subscription, service Usage, and service Chargeback as applicable

(Syllabus Reference: Unit 3, Basic Concepts, Learning Outcome 15: You should be able to list the R2F typical activities.)

There are four typical activities in the R2F Value Stream:

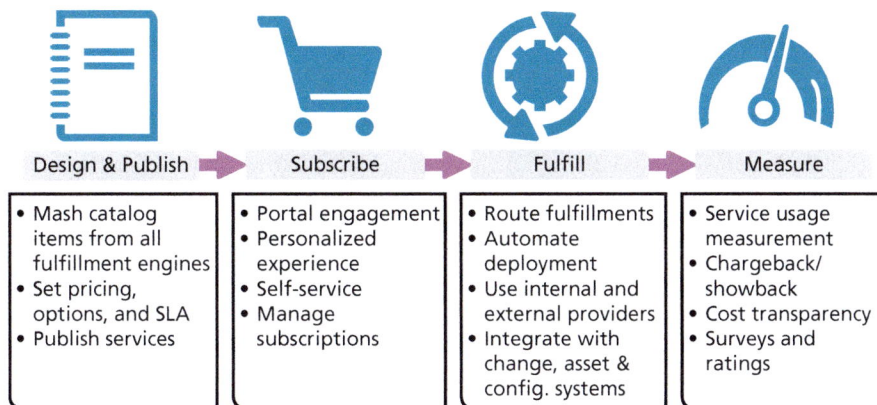

Figure 8:   Request to Fulfill Activities

Design & Publish
This activity focuses on the creation of a catalog, the definition of the various service terms, and laying the foundation for the consumption of IT services. All the catalog items and products are combined ("mashed") into a single unified catalog, pricing options are set, and the unified catalog published in the form of offers.

Subscribe
A consistent and personalized experience is provided, so that users can manage Subscriptions through a self-service model. This enables the users to request services, and to manage them and their associated Subscriptions throughout the lifecycle.

Fulfill
This delivers the request; this may include orchestration across multiple fulfillment engines and providers. This includes routing fulfillment requests and automated deployment.

Measure
Actual usage of service is measured, and costs are made available in the form of Chargebacks and Showbacks. This provides information to the consumer

or owners helping them to manage their Subscriptions and control the spending.

4.5 The Detect to Correct (D2C) Value Stream

(Syllabus Reference: Unit 3, Basic Concepts, Learning Outcome 16: You should be able to describe the scope of the D2C Value Stream.)

The Detect to Correct (D2C) Value Stream provides a framework for integrating the monitoring, management, remediation, and other operational aspects associated with realized services and/or those under construction. It also provides a comprehensive overview of the business of IT operations and the services that these teams deliver.

Anchored by the Service Model, the D2C Value Stream delivers new levels of insight into the inter-dependencies that exist among the various operational domains; including Event, Incident, Problem, Change Control, and Configuration Management. It also provides the business context for operational requests and new requirements. The D2C Value Stream is designed to accommodate a variety of sourcing methodologies across services, technologies, and functions. This value stream makes clear the inter-relationships required to fix operational issues. It supports IT business objectives of greater agility, improved uptime, and lower cost per service.

The D2C Value Stream provides a framework for bringing IT service operations functions together to enhance IT results and efficiencies. Generally, data is not shared between IT domains either because they do not understand which key data objects to share, or because they do not have a common language for sharing. When projects are created to improve data sharing, they are often too difficult and cumbersome to finish, or an internal technology or organization shift may occur that invalidates the result.

The D2C Value Stream defines the functional components and the data that needs to flow between components. This is needed to enhance a business and service-oriented approach to maintenance, and facilitates data flow to the other value streams.

(Syllabus Reference: Unit 3, Basic Concepts, Learning Outcome 17: You should be able to list the D2C value propositions.)

The key value propositions for adopting the D2C Value Stream are to:
- Identify and prioritize issues in a timely fashion
- Improve data sharing to accelerate the ability to understand the business impact
- Automate both within domains and across domains
- Ensure the development of an operating model, capabilities, and processes that can handle the complexity of service delivery across multiple internal and external domains
- Effectively link Events to Incidents to Problems to Defects in the R2D Value Stream

(Syllabus Reference: Unit 3, Basic Concepts, Learning Outcome 18: You should be able to list the D2C typical activities.)

Typical activities include:

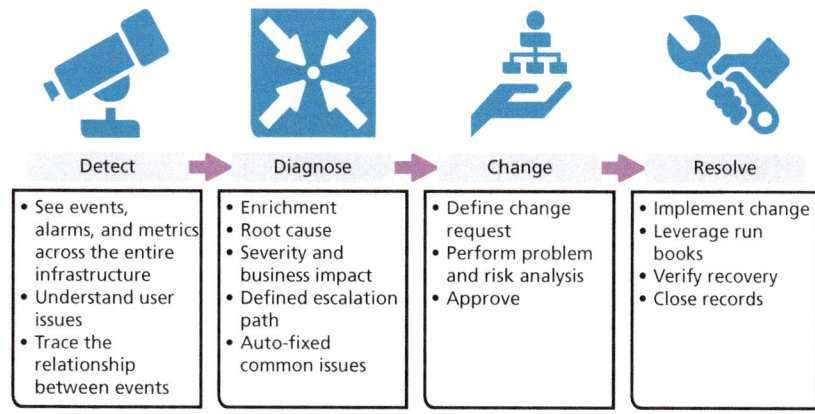

Figure 9: Detect to Correct Activities

Detect
This includes early identification of anomalies across the IT ecosystem. This is not limited only to servers that are on the local premises; it can include cloud servers and storage servers. If a condition is important, then when it is detected it generates a notification – called an Event. Events are sent to the diagnostic system.

Diagnose
This gathers all information around the Event to determine if it is real, and attempts to identify the root cause. If a service is interrupted we want to automatically restore or have defined steps put underway.

Change
Based on the Event it may be determined that some change is required to prevent a reoccurrence. This change will be reviewed and approved.

Resolve
This is where the implementation of a change occurs. A Run Book, which is an automated mechanism, is the preferable way to implement the change.

4.6 The IT4IT Reference Architecture

The IT Value Chain is supported by the IT4IT Reference Architecture. The IT4IT Reference Architecture provides a prescriptive framework to support the value chain-based IT organization and service-centric IT management ecosystem.

(Syllabus Reference: Unit 3, Basic Concepts, Learning Outcome 19: You should be able to explain the concept of the four pillars "anchoring" the IT Value Chain – the Service Model, the Information Model, the Functional Model, and the Integration Model.)

Previous approaches for creating a reference architecture in the IT management domain have been oriented around processes, capabilities, and technology implementations. Unfortunately, processes can be implemented differently for each IT organizational archetype and capabilities are largely influenced by technology implementations. As a result, this architecture approach often results in a complex mesh of products and solutions requiring countless point-to-point integrations to accommodate the variations in process.

The IT4IT Reference Architecture approach for the IT Value Chain is anchored by four pillars – the Service Model, the Information Model, the Functional Model, and the Integration Model. These areas, when captured and modeled correctly, remain constant regardless of changes to process, technology, and/or capabilities.

4.6.1 The Service Model

(Syllabus Reference: Unit 3, Basic Concepts, Learning Outcome 20: You should be able to explain the IT4IT Service Model.)

The Service Model construct in the architecture captures, connects, and maintains service lifecycle attributes as the service progresses through its lifecycle. The IT4IT Service Model's provider/broker model focuses on services as the primary IT deliverable and requires a higher degree of flexibility, velocity, and adaptability. A service-centric lifecycle framework is one that supports a continuous cycle of portfolio assessment, sourcing and integration of components, and service offering to consumers.

(Syllabus Reference: Unit 3, Basic Concepts, Learning Outcome 21: You should be able to describe the Service Model Backbone.)

The structure that binds the different abstraction levels of the Service Model together is called the "Service Model Backbone" (shown in Figure 10). The Service Model Backbone provides the data entities, attributes, and the necessary relationships between them, to ensure end-to-end traceability of a service from the initial concept to instantiation and consumption.

This data-driven, model-based approach will ensure that the required service is actually what gets delivered or, in other words, the offered service will produce the outcome that the consumer desires. It also allows the IT organization to utilize a service-centric approach to create and package its deliverables.

The Service Model Backbone requires the creation of services from across resource and capability domains such as infrastructure, application components, database, middleware, monitoring, and support. This enables the organization to improve their speed and consistency through higher re-use of pre-existing services and to embrace new technologies such as containers and micro-services more effectively.

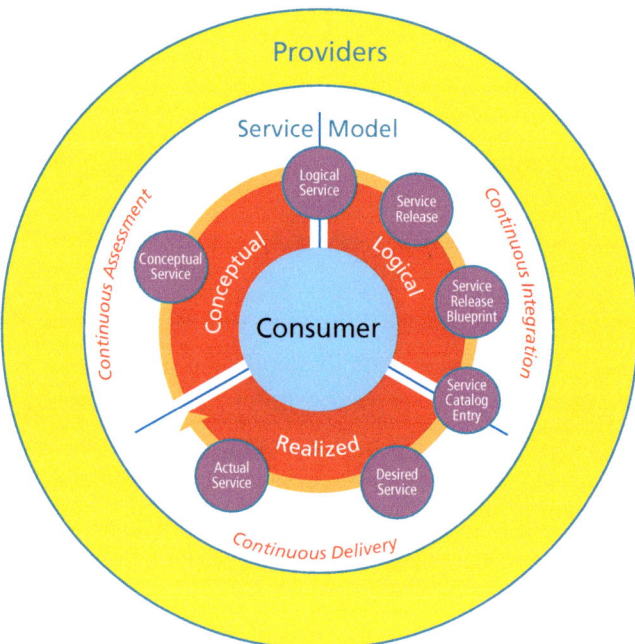

Figure 10: IT4IT Service Model

4.6.2 The IT4IT Information Model

(Syllabus Reference: Unit 3, Basic Concepts, Learning Outcome 22: You should be able to describe the IT4IT Information Model.)

The Information Model comprises the set of service lifecycle data objects and their relationships.

Taken together, the data produced and/or consumed by the value streams represents all of the information required to control the activities that advance a service through its lifecycle. This data is referred to as the "service lifecycle *data objects*" (data objects in short form). Some data objects contribute directly to creating and/or advancing the Service Model, while others serve as connectors, providing the linkage between functional components and across value streams.

(Syllabus Reference: Unit 3, Basic Concepts, Learning Outcome 23: You should be able to state the characteristics of service lifecycle data objects.)

Service lifecycle data objects have the following characteristics:
- They describe an aspect of a service

- They are inputs or outputs associated with an IT4IT functional component or a service lifecycle phase
- They are uniquely identified, and have a lifecycle of their own
- They maintain structured information that allows for relationship tracking and automation

(Syllabus Reference: Unit 3, Basic Concepts, Learning Outcome 24: You should be able to explain the difference between key and auxiliary data objects.)

Service lifecycle data objects are grouped into two categories: key and auxiliary.

Data Object Type	Description	Symbol
Key Data Objects	Key data objects describe "how" services are created, delivered, and consumed; they are essential to managing the service lifecycle. Managing the end-to-end service lifecycle and associated measurement, reporting, and traceability would be virtually impossible without them. The IT4IT Reference Architecture defines 32 key data objects and most are depicted as black circles.	●
	Service models are a stand-alone subclass of key data objects that describe "what" IT delivers to its consumers. They represent the attributes of a service at three levels of abstraction: Conceptual, Logical, and Realized. These data objects are referred to as Service Model Backbone data objects (or Service Backbone data objects in short form) and depicted using a purple colored circle in the IT4IT Reference Architecture diagrams. Note that the Logical Service Model is subdivided into a Design part, a Release part, and a Consumable part. Similarly, the Realized data object is represented with both a Desired and an Actual model part.	●
Auxiliary Data Objects	Auxiliary data objects provide context for the "why, when, where, etc." attributes and, while they are important to the IT function, they *do not play a vital role in managing the service lifecycle*. The IT4IT Reference Architecture currently describes eight (8) auxiliary data objects and they are depicted using a gray colored circle.	●

4.6.3 The IT4IT Functional Model

(Syllabus Reference: Unit 3, Basic Concepts, Learning Outcome 25: You should be able to state what the IT4IT Functional Model is.)

The IT4IT Reference Architecture identifies and defines essential building blocks – known as functional components – which create or consume data objects and are aligned with the value streams of the IT Value Chain. The IT4IT Functional Model is the set of functional components and their relationships.

(Syllabus Reference: Unit 3, Basic Concepts, Learning Outcome 26: You should be able to explain functional components and how they relate to IT capability.)

The context for functional components starts with an IT "capability". A capability is the ability that an organization, person, or system possesses (i.e., the function or activity it can perform) which produces an outcome of value through the utilization of a combination of people, process, methods, technology resources, and/or tools.

Functional components can be logically associated to IT capabilities for organizational clarity and should be underpinned with processes to drive uniformity and consistency.

While the definition of capabilities is used as a context for defining functional components, they are not the central focus within the IT4IT Reference Architecture. The documentation only refers to capabilities if there is a non-core capability that interacts with the architecture. In that case, using capability reduces the need to provide details for functional components and data objects that are outside the scope of the IT4IT Reference Architecture (for example, IT Financial Management).

Capabilities are supported by "building blocks" called functional components. A grouping of one or more functional components represents the technology elements of an IT capability.

4.6.4 Functional Components

(Syllabus Reference: Unit 3, Basic Concepts, Learning Outcome 27: You should be able to understand the difference between primary functional components and secondary functional components.)

Functional components are grouped into two categories: *primary* and *secondary*.

Functional Component Type	Description	Symbol
Primary Functional Component (sometimes also known as key)	A primary functional component plays a key role in the activities of a specific value stream. Without this functional component, the integrity of the data objects, and thus the Service Model, could not be maintained consistently and efficiently. The IT4IT documentation describes primary functional components as being owned by, or core to, a particular value stream.	▇
Secondary Functional Component (sometimes also known as auxiliary)	Secondary functional components have some level of dependency or interaction with a value stream and its data objects. While they interact with a value stream, secondary functional components are not core to it, and are either primary to another value stream or supporting function, or represent a capability.	▇

4.6.5 Functional Components and Data Objects

(Syllabus Reference: Unit 3, Basic Concepts, Learning Outcome 28: You should be able to explain interactions between functional components and data objects.)

The relationships and dependencies between the data objects controlled by functional components are depicted using a solid line along with cardinality mapping (e.g., 1:1). In addition to the entity relationships, functional components interact and exchange data to form the relationship. The data exchange between functional components is depicted using a dotted-line arrow, which represents the direction of the flow (see Figure 11).

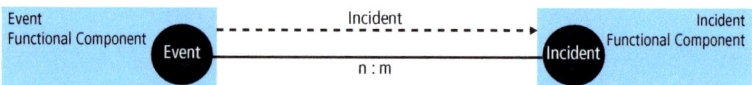

Figure 11: Data Flows in the IT4IT Reference Architecture

Although the IT4IT Reference Architecture depicts data flow and relationships between functional components, it does not advocate or prescribe processes that make this happen. The IT4IT Reference Architecture is process-agnostic in that it provides a prescriptive framework, which remains constant regardless of whether an organization utilizes ITIL, COBIT, eTOM, or internally developed processes.

4.6.6 The IT4IT Integration Model

 Details of the IT4T Integration Model are beyond the scope of the IT4IT Foundation syllabus. A brief summary is included here.

The IT4IT Reference Architecture defines an integration model composed of three types of integrations for simplifying the creation of an IT management ecosystem using functional components.

System of Record Integrations
These entity relationship definitions ensure the consistent management of the lifecycle for individual data objects, as well as ensuring that the data objects are consistently named and cross-linked through prescriptive data flows between functional components to maintain the integrity of the Service Model. In the Level 2 notation (see Section 5.4), these are depicted using a dotted black line.

System of Engagement Integrations
These are user interface integrations derived from value stream use-cases and user stories. These integrations deliver the technology underpinning for a capability by combining several functional components into a single user experience to facilitate human interaction with data objects. In the Level 2 notation, these are depicted using a dotted blue line.

System of Insight Integrations

These include intelligence, analytics, and KPI-centric integrations. The notation for this integration type has not yet been defined and is reserved for future use.

4.6.7 IT Service

(Syllabus Reference: Unit 3, Basic Concepts, Learning Outcome 29: You should be able to explain IT service.)

An IT service is a performance of an act that applies computing and information management competencies or resources for the benefit of another party. Every IT service has three aspects:

- The Service Interaction: the interaction between provider and consumer
- The Service Offer: the offer that exposes the value proposition to consumers
- The Service System: the people, process, and technology that facilitate the outcome

These three aspects are summarized in Figure 12.

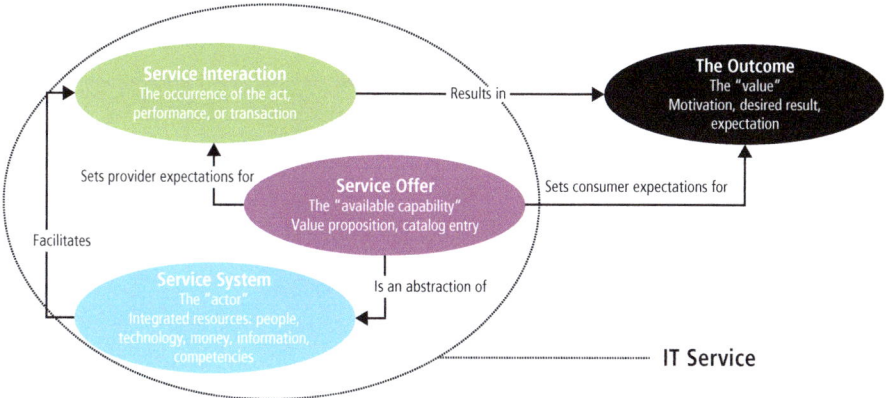

Figure 12:   IT Service

4.7 Summary

This chapter has described the scope, value propositions, and typical activities of the four value streams, as well as the basic concepts of the IT4IT Reference

Architecture, including the Service Model, the Information Model, the Functional Model, the Integration Model, and IT Service.

4.8 Recommended Reading

The following are recommended sources of further information for this chapter:
- The IT4IT Reference Architecture, Version 2.1, Chapter 3

4.9 Exercise 3: Basic Concepts

In your own words, provide short answers to these questions.

1. What is the scope of the Strategy to Portfolio Value Stream?

2. What is the scope of the Requirement to Deploy Value Stream?

3. What is the scope of the Request to Fulfill Value Stream?

4. What is the scope of the Detect to Correct Value Stream?

5. What are the typical activities of each value stream?

6. What is the IT4IT Service Model?

7. What is the Service Model Backbone?

8. What is the IT4IT Information Model?

9. What is the IT4IT Functional Model?
   _____
   _____

10. What is the difference between primary functional components and secondary functional components?
    _____
    _____

4.10 Test Yourself Questions

Q1: What is the scope of the S2P Value Stream?
   A. It is focused on creating, building, or sourcing new services, or modifying those that exist.
   B. It is focused on connecting consumers with the goods and services used to satisfy productivity and innovation needs.
   C. It is focused on operational aspects associated with realized services and those under construction.
   D. It is focused on managing the portfolio of services delivered to the enterprise.

Q2: Which value stream has the four typical activities: plan & design, develop, test, deploy?
   A. D2C
   B. R2D
   C. R2F
   D. S2P

Q3: What is a key value proposition for the R2F Value Stream?
   A. Ensure that the Service Release meets business expectations.
   B. Establish a holistic view so that IT portfolio decisions are based on business priorities.
   C. Facilitate a holistic view across service Subscription, Usage, and Chargeback.
   D. Timely identification of an issue.

Q4: Which value stream receives the Conceptual Service and enables development of the Logical Service?
A. Detect to Correct
B. Request to Fulfill
C. Requirement to Deploy
D. Strategy to Portfolio

Q5: Complete the sentence: The purpose of the Detect to Correct Value Stream is to _____.
A. bring together IT service operations functions for greater efficiency
B. build what the business needs, when it needs it, ensuring it meets business expectations
C. catalog, fulfill, and manage service usage, providing consistency
D. drive portfolio to business innovation, placing emphasis on the service delivered

Q6: What construct in the architecture captures, connects, and maintains service lifecycle attributes as the service progresses through its lifecycle?
A. The Functional Model
B. The IT4IT Information Model
C. The Integration Model
D. The Service Model

Q7: What are uniquely identified, have a lifecycle of their own, and are inputs or outputs associated with a functional component?
A. Relationships
B. Secondary functional components
C. Service lifecycle data objects
D. Value streams

Q8: The IT4IT Reference Architecture describes eight of these; they do not play a vital role in managing the service lifecycle; they are depicted using a gray colored circle. What are they?
A. Auxiliary data objects
B. Key data objects
C. Primary functional components
D. Secondary functional components

Chapter 5

IT4IT Core

5.1 Key Learning Points

This chapter will help you understand the IT4IT Reference Architecture at a high level.

Key Points Explained
This chapter introduces the following:
- The five abstraction levels of the IT4IT Reference Architecture
- The Level 1 IT4IT Reference Architecture
- The concepts for Abstraction Level 2
- The concepts for Abstraction Level 3
- An overview of Abstraction Levels 4 and 5

5.2 IT4IT Abstractions

(Syllabus Reference: Unit 4, IT4IT Core, Learning Outcome 1: You should be able to list the five levels of IT4IT abstractions and identify which are vendor-agnostic and which are vendor-specific.)

The IT4IT Reference Architecture is communicated using multiple levels of abstraction. This approach has been taken to ensure that the Reference Architecture is consumable, even if you are not an architect. On the other hand it is precise, specific, and complete end-to-end. This is similar to the approach employed by other frameworks, such as the Business Process Framework (eTOM) from the TM Forum.

Each abstraction level expands on the prior to expose more details and prescriptive guidance. The upper levels (1-3) are vendor-agnostic, and provide generic views that are suitable both for strategy and planning purposes as well as creating IT management product roadmaps.

The lower levels (4-5) provide more specific details, ultimately arriving at implementation level or vendor-owned/controlled information. Content at these levels is suitable for developing implementation plans and for facilitating product design. The IT4IT Reference Architecture defines five abstraction levels as follows:

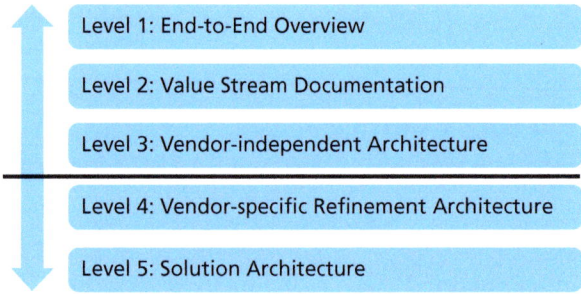

Figure 13: IT4IT Reference Architecture Levels

Level 1 is an overview level; an abstraction that allows all the concepts of the Reference Architecture to be seen in a single slide. Using a simplified informal notation with only three symbols, it provides a holistic model of the IT4IT Reference Architecture. It introduces the core terms and concepts, which underpin the architecture, and depicts the high-level foundation controls that an IT organization needs in place to standardize, automate, and manage the IT Value Chain.

Level 2 describes each of the value streams in simple terms, and starts to describe the flow of information.

Level 3 describes the comprehensive normative Reference Architecture in a formal notation, expressed in the ArchiMate modeling language or UML terms.

Levels 4 and 5 are vendor-specific, and interoperability is achieved by the presence of Level 3.

(Syllabus Reference: Unit 4, IT4IT Core, Learning Outcome 2: You should be able to explain why an informal notation was chosen for Levels 1 and 2.)

Levels 1 and 2 use a simplified class model and an informal notation to introduce and explain concepts. An informal notation was selected at these levels so that non-architects would easily understand the architecture.

Level 3 and below are more applicable to architects, and thus the formal notation is the preferred means of communicating concepts at this level. The IT4IT Reference Architecture focuses on documenting and governing Levels 1 to 3. Levels 4 and 5 are controlled by product and service providers or potentially other forums, and the IT4IT Reference Architecture merely provides exemplar guidance at these levels.

5.3 Level 1 Concepts

(Syllabus Reference: Unit 4, IT4IT Core, Learning Outcome 3: You should be able to list the five core concepts introduced at Reference Architecture Level 1.)

At this level, the five core concepts of the IT4IT Reference Architecture are introduced:
- Value streams
- Functional components
- Service lifecycle data objects (key data objects)
- Service Model Backbone data objects (Service Backbone data objects)
- Relationships

(Syllabus Reference: Unit 4, IT4IT Core, Learning Outcome 4: You should be able to explain the Level 1 class model.)

The inter-relationships of these five concepts are shown in Figure 14. (Note that the graphic uses UML notation to depict the multiplicity.)

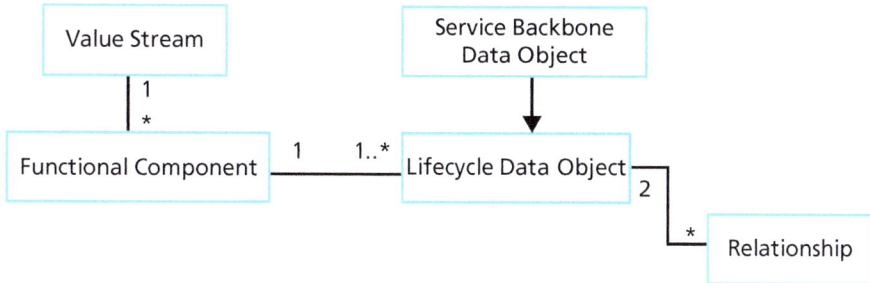

Figure 14: Level 1 Class Model

An important point to understand from the class model in Figure 14 is that both types of data objects are considered service lifecycle data objects (see Section 3.2.1). This means that the "Service Backbone data objects" that are used to represent the Service Model are a type of lifecycle data object. The IT4IT standard treats Service Backbone data objects differently because they play a special role in the Reference Architecture.

Also notice that capability is missing from the diagram. While capability mapping remains an important activity for IT organizations, it is not included as part of the normative documentation. Instead, other documents (guidance documents) will provide this level of detail.

Figure 15 shows a section from the Level 1 Reference Architecture diagram and highlights the core concepts. The black circle is a data object – known formally as a service lifecycle data object or key data object. The blue rectangle is a functional component. Each functional component should control one data object. The Level 1 architecture identifies 33 data objects (32 of which are key data objects). The black lines show the relationships between the data objects; for example, an incident is related to an event and *vice versa*. Some of the key data objects keep track of the real Service Model, and are shown in the IT4IT standard in a different color – purple.

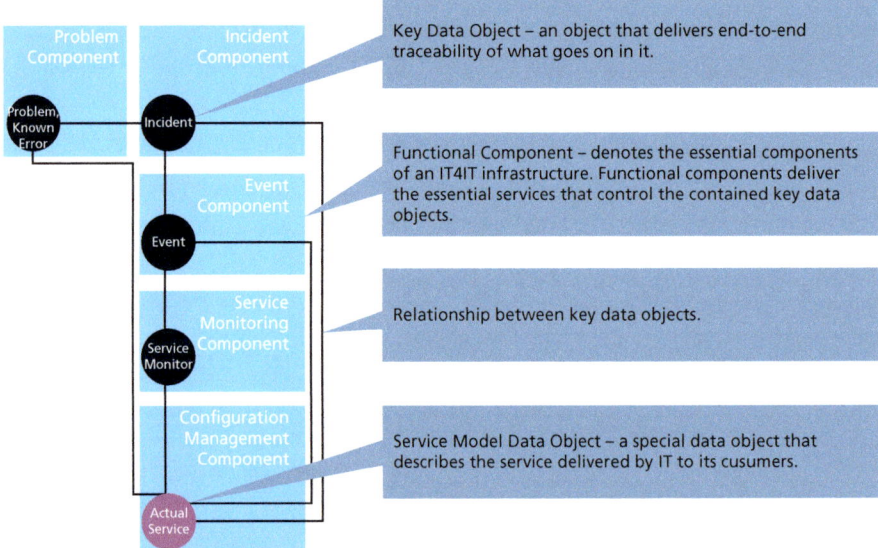

Figure 15: Level 1 Concepts

(Syllabus Reference: Unit 4, IT4IT Core, Learning Outcome 5: You should be able to explain the objective of the IT4IT Reference Architecture as it relates to Level 1.)

The objective of the IT4IT Reference Architecture is to convey, in a prescriptive fashion, the key data objects, relationships, and components that are foundational for all IT organizations.

5.3.1 Value Streams

(Syllabus Reference: Unit 4, IT4IT Core, Learning Outcome 6: You should be able to explain how the IT4IT Reference Architecture uses the value stream concept.)

The IT4IT Reference Architecture uses the value stream concept as a way of grouping the functional components and data objects together to provide context for where value is being created/delivered.

5.3.2 Functional Components

(Syllabus Reference: Unit 4, IT4IT Core, Learning Outcome 7: You should be able to list the three things a functional component must have.)

A functional component (shown as a blue rectangle in the Level 1 notation) is the smallest unit of technology that can stand on its own and be useful as a whole to an IT practitioner or IT service provider.

Functional components must have defined input(s) and output(s) that are data objects and must have an impact on a key data object; for example, create, update, or delete. Typically, a functional component controls and/or manages a single type of data object but this is not dictated by the architecture.

In the IT4IT Reference Architecture, functional components are aligned with specific value streams and supporting functions. The components aligned with a given value stream are considered to be its "primary" functional components. Functional components that affect key data objects for a given value stream but aren't primary to that value stream are considered "secondary" functional components. The Reference Architecture uses different colors to distinguish between primary and secondary functional components (see Section 4.6.2).

5.3.3 Service Lifecycle Data Objects

A service lifecycle data object (lifecycle data object) represents data (records, information, and so on) that annotate or model an aspect of a service being offered by IT. Data objects can take a digital or physical form and can be comprised of structured, semi-structured, or unstructured data. Examples of data objects include incident records, training videos, requirements documents, project plans, etc.

(Syllabus Reference: Unit 4, IT4IT Core, Learning Outcome 8: You should be able to identify the OMG definition that is aligned contextually with the service lifecycle data object (artifact).)

The definition of service lifecycle data object is aligned contextually with the OMG definition of an artifact.

In UML, the OMG defines "artifact" as:

"... the specification of a physical piece of information that is used or produced by a software development process, or by deployment and operation of a system. Examples of artifacts include model files, source files, scripts, and binary executable files, a table in a database system, a development deliverable, or a word-processing document, a mail message."

5.3.4 Relationships

(Syllabus Reference: Unit 4, IT4IT Core, Learning Outcome 9: You should be able to identify the constituent parts of the system of record fabric for IT management.)

An important aspect of the IT4IT Reference Architecture is defining not only the data objects, but the essential relationships between them. Figure 16 is a view of the Level 1 Reference Architecture (see Figure 17) with the functional components removed, highlighting the essential data objects and relationships. The data objects, combined with their relationships and interdependencies, form the "system of record fabric" for IT management. These relationships are referred to as system of record integrations (record-centric, SoR in short form).

The system of record fabric is shown in Figure 16. Its constituent parts are as follows:
- The black circles denote data objects – known as service lifecycle data objects or key data objects
- The solid lines show the relationships between the data objects; for example, a problem is related to an incident and *vice versa*; a Service Model data object (shown in purple in the IT4IT Reference Architecture) is a special data object that describes the service delivered by IT to its consumers
- Auxiliary data objects (shown in gray) provide context for the "why, when, where, etc." attributes and, while they are important to the IT function, they do not play a vital role in managing the service lifecycle

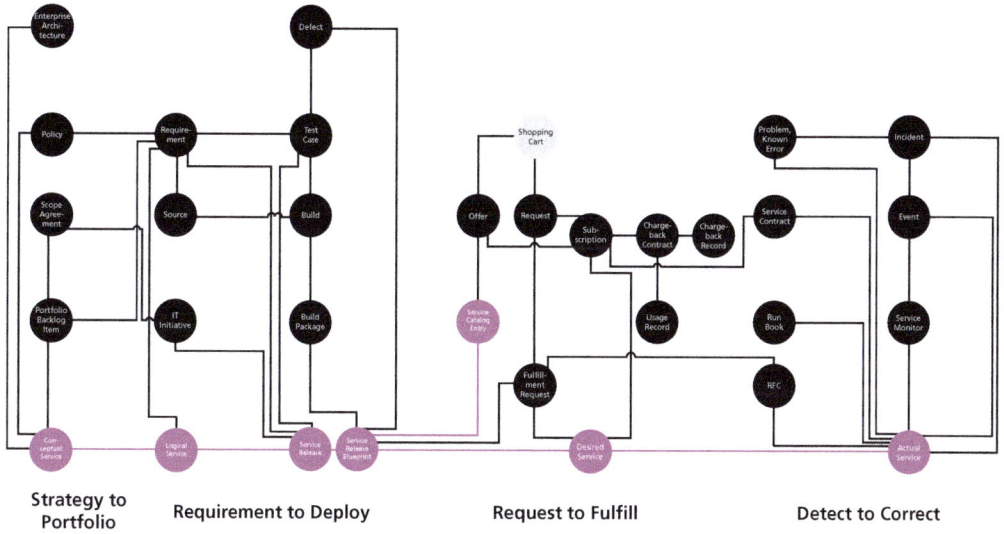

Figure 16:   System of Record Fabric

5.3.5 Level 1 Reference Architecture Model
(Syllabus Reference: Unit 4, IT4IT Core, Learning Outcome 10: You should be able to briefly explain the Level 1 Reference Architecture.)

Figure 17 shows the Level 1 model for the IT4IT Reference Architecture. The four value streams from the IT Value Chain are shown along the bottom of the diagram. The blue rectangles are the functional components that act on

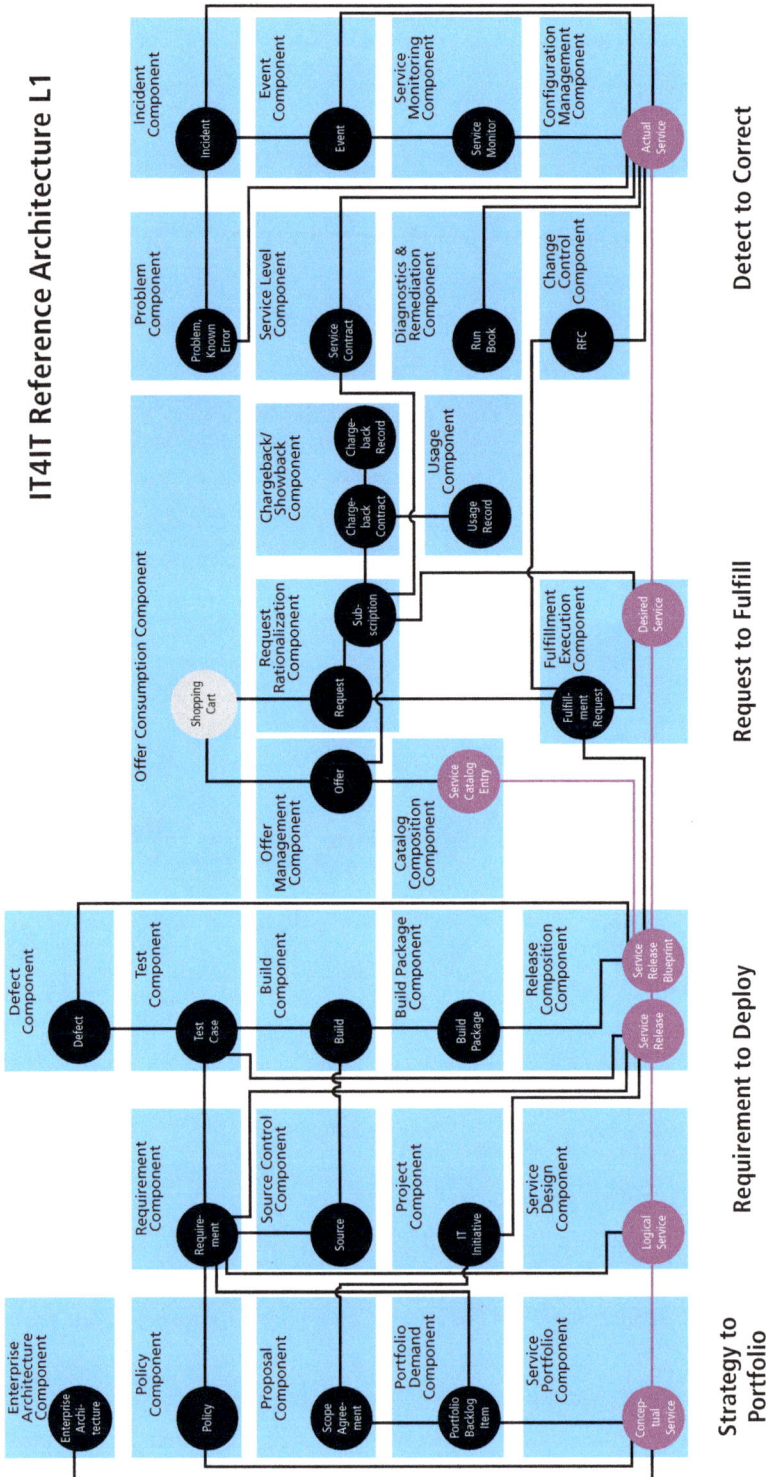

Figure 17: IT4IT Level 1 Reference Architecture Model

the artifacts (the lifecycle data objects), which are shown as black circles. The artifacts are connected by solid lines, which are the relationships between the data objects.

The Service Model data objects are shown as purple circles in the IT4IT Reference Architecture. The line linking these shows the stages of the service definition, and is known as the Service Backbone – it is what provides traceability. It shows how you can trace from a Conceptual Service to a Logical Service, through to a Desired Service and then to an Actual Service in production. You can go all the way from a Conceptual Service and determine what has been done, where is it in development, which data center has installations of this, and how many incidents are being created on which versions of that Conceptual Service.

5.4 Level 2 Concepts

(Syllabus Reference: Unit 4, IT4IT Core, Learning Outcome 11: You should be able to list the four additional concepts at Reference Architecture Level 2.)

Abstraction at Level 2 expands on the concepts introduced in Level 1, providing definitions and details and introducing a few more concepts, including:
- Relationships between data objects are updated with multiplicity/cardinality attributes (e.g., one-to-one, one-to-many, many-to-many)
- The concept of data flow between functional components is introduced
- The data flows are refined to depict integrations to build out the system of record fabric
- The relationships between capability disciplines and functional components are introduced but they are not part of the normative Reference Architecture and are presented as guidance

(Syllabus Reference: Unit 4, IT4IT Core, Learning Outcome 12: You should be able to explain the Level 2 class model.)

For Level 2, the Level 1 class diagram in Figure 14 is expanded to reflect these additions, as shown in Figure 18.

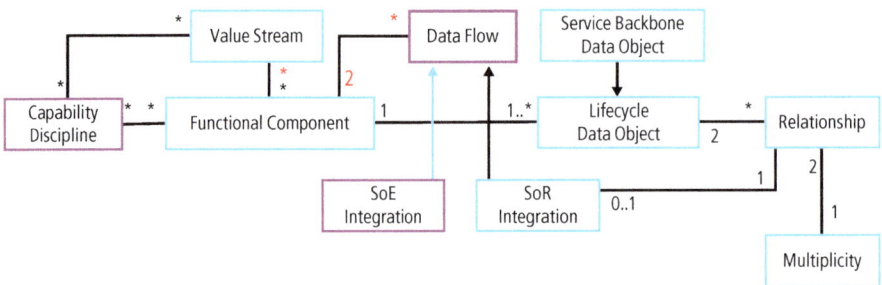

Figure 18:   Level 2 Class Model

The Level 2 concepts are communicated through a set of normative documents and simplified views into the definitive vendor-independent model maintained at Level 3.

5.4.1 Level 2 Reference Architecture Diagram (Example)
(Syllabus Reference: Unit 4, IT4IT Core, Learning Outcome 13: You should be able to briefly explain an example Level 2 Reference Architecture diagram.)

Figure 19 provides an example of a Level 2 model/diagram using the informal notation. This example is the Strategy to Portfolio (S2P) Value Stream and this graphic represents the content contained in abstraction Level 2. At this level there is more detail on the data relationships and the data flow between functional components, including the cardinality. Functional components that are from another value stream (for example, the Service Design functional component from the R2D Value Stream) or that are supporting functions (for example, IT Asset Management) are depicted in the IT4IT Reference Architecture as gray-green rectangles.

5.5 Level 3 Concepts
(Syllabus Reference: Unit 4, IT4IT Core, Learning Outcome 14: You should be able to identify the primary method for communicating the IT4IT Reference Architecture at Level 3.)

A formal notation is the primary method for communicating the IT4IT Reference Architecture specification at abstraction Level 3. The notations used include both the ArchiMate language and UML.

Ch. 5 IT4IT CORE

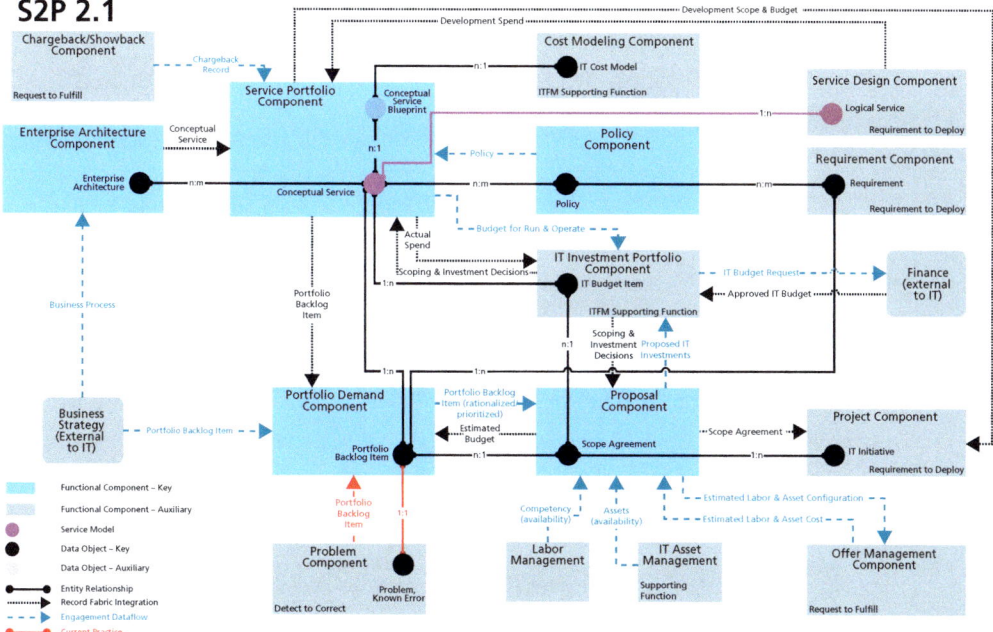

Figure 19: Example Level 2 Diagram (S2P Value Stream)

(Syllabus Reference: Unit 4, IT4IT Core, Learning Outcome 15: You should be able to list the additional concepts introduced at Reference Architecture Level 3.)

This level adds more details for data object definitions, introducing essential attributes for key data objects. It also introduces the concepts of scenarios and essential services. Figure 20 shows the additions to the IT4IT Reference Architecture class model at Level 3.

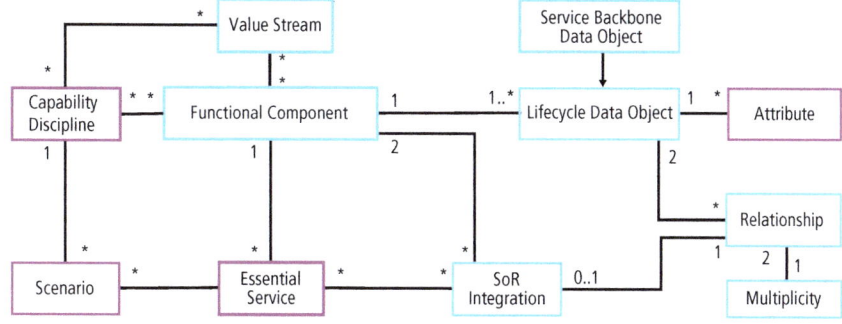

Figure 20: Level 3 Class Model

As described in Levels 1 and 2, data objects represent the data exchanged between functional components. At abstraction Level 3, the essential attributes of objects that must be present in the exchange are also specified. UML is the notation chosen for essential attributes.

(Syllabus Reference: Unit 4, IT4IT Core, Learning Outcome 16: You should be able to identify the notation used for the Level 3 Reference Architecture diagrams.)

The ArchiMate notation guidelines used in Level 3 are shown in Figure 21. Where constructs are used for multiple purposes the name reflects how it is being used. For example, the Business Function construct is used to represent Value Chain, Value Stream, and Capability Discipline and when this happens the name will reflect which entity is represented.

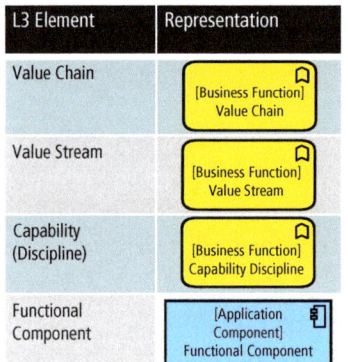
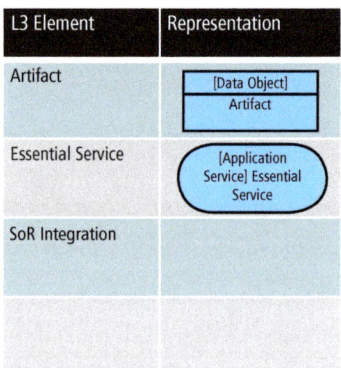

Figure 21: Level 3 Notation Guide

5.6 Levels 4 and 5

(Syllabus Reference: Unit 4, IT4IT Core, Learning Outcome 17: You should be able to explain who owns and controls Levels 4 and 5 of Reference Architecture.)

Levels 4 and 5 are owned and controlled by suppliers of IT management products and services. The IT4IT Reference Architecture has no direct control over defining and/or approving content at these abstraction levels. What is provided in this section of the standard are recommendations and examples of typical elements at these levels.

For example, vendors might add essential services to the baseline or add functional components to differentiate their product or offering. The principle to be applied here is that whatever is added should build from and not change the prescriptive model defined in Levels 1 to 3.

(Syllabus Reference: Unit 4, IT4IT Core, Learning Outcome 18: You should be able to explain what kind of content might be included in Level 4.)

Abstraction Level 4 is where the architecture becomes more product-design and implementation-oriented. Here, for example, providers of IT management products and services can design/specify their service, interface, and exchange models that should be derived from Level 3 content. Other examples of Level 4 content might include:

- Defining extensions to the standard – *"these essential attributes are being used, and these are added for the following reasons …"*
- Adding data objects – *"these non-key data objects were added, and are using the same notation style to reflect how they build off the baseline architecture"*
- Additional notations – *"the ArchiMate language is used for explaining scenarios and UML for the data models"*
- Introduction of process – might introduce/model practitioner-level processes within scenarios
- Canonical data model – might introduce the vendor-specific canonical data model for their IT management products
- Integrations – might specify the techniques/methods used in implementing system of record integrations

Regardless of the how the vendor chooses to adapt and implement the architecture, it must be able to be mapped back into what is specified at Levels 1 to 3.

(Syllabus Reference: Unit 4, IT4IT Core, Learning Outcome 19: You should be able to explain what kind of content might be included in Level 5.)

Abstraction Level 5 provides vendor-specific representations for an implementation of part or all of the Reference Architecture. It is the level at which the specifications and/or functionality for IT management products

and services are provided. Deviations and adaptations to the Reference Architecture are also documented here. Examples of content at Level 5 might include:
- The structure used by vendor X to implement the D2C Value Stream
- Vendor Y uses the "timestamp" essential attribute on the Event data object but names it "timeofday"
- Vendor Z uses a product called ServiceXchange as the platform for essential services

Notation and naming at Level 5 is vendor-owned/controlled but should reflect adherence to the baseline architecture and prescriptive guidance in Levels 1 to 3.

5.7 Summary

This chapter has described the five abstraction levels of the IT4IT Reference Architecture and the key concepts of each level. Level 1 is an Overview level – the Reference Architecture in a single slide. Level 2 describes each of the value streams in simple terms. Level 3 describes the full Reference Architecture in a formal notation and is where interoperability is achieved. Levels 4 and 5 are vendor-specific.

5.8 Recommended Reading

The following are recommended sources of further information for this chapter:
- The IT4IT Reference Architecture, Version 2.1, Chapter 4
- IT4IT Reference Architecture, Version 2.1 Reference Cards

5.9 Exercise 4: IT4IT Core

1. Insert the number (1..5) in the Answer column to match the IT4IT Reference Architecture Level:

Answer	Abstraction Level Description
_____	Solution Architecture
_____	Value Stream Documentation

Answer	Abstraction Level Description
_____	End-to-End Overview
_____	Vendor-specific Refinement Architecture
_____	Vendor-independent Architecture

2. Why was an informal notation chosen for Levels 1 and 2 of the Reference Architecture?

3. What are the five core concepts introduced at Level 1 of the Reference Architecture?

4. What is the objective of the representation of the Level 1 IT4IT Reference Architecture?

5. How does the IT4IT Reference Architecture use the value stream concept?

6. What are the four additional concepts introduced at Reference Architecture Level 2?

7. What are the additional concepts introduced at Reference Architecture Level 3?

8. What is the notation used for the Level 3 Reference Architecture diagrams?

9. Who owns and controls Levels 4 and 5 of the Reference Architecture?

10. What kind of content might be included in Level 4 of the Reference Architecture?

_____

_____

5.10 Test Yourself Questions

Q1: Which of the IT4IT Reference Architecture abstraction levels are vendor-agnostic?
   A. The lower levels (4-5)
   B. The middle levels (2-4)
   C. The outer levels (1,5)
   D. The upper levels (1-3)

Q2: Which of the IT4IT Reference Architecture abstraction levels use an informal notation to introduce and explain the concepts?
   A. Level 3 and below
   B. Levels 1 and 2
   C. The upper levels (1-3)
   D. Levels 4 and 5

Q3: Complete the sentence: In a Level 2 Reference Architecture diagram the gray-green rectangles represent _____.
   A. capability discipline objects
   B. functional components from another value stream
   C. lifecycle data objects
   D. Service Model Backbone data objects

Q4: What are the three things that a functional component must have?
   A. A unique identity, one data object, and experience-centric integration
   B. Inputs, outputs, and an impact on a key data object
   C. Intelligence, analytics, and KPI-centric integrations
   D. One or more relationships, a capability discipline, and a scenario

Q5: What OMG UML definition is aligned with the service lifecycle data object?
   A. Artifact

B. Catalog
C. Model
D. Work Product

Q6: In the Level 1 Reference Architecture diagram, what does the horizontal line linking the circles along the bottom represent?
A. The Conceptual Service
B. The lifecycle data objects
C. The Service Model Backbone
D. The system of record fabric

Q7: In the Level 2 class model, what does the Reference Architecture introduce between functional components?
A. Data flow
B. Linkage
C. Relationships
D. Service lifecycle data objects

Q8: What is the notation used for the Level 3 Reference Architecture diagrams?
A. ArchiMate language and UML
B. BPMN
C. IDEF0
D. xBML

Chapter 6

The Strategy to Portfolio Value Stream

6.1 Key Learning Points

This chapter will help you understand the Strategy to Portfolio Value Stream.

Key Points Explained

This chapter will help you to understand and explain:
- The objectives of the value stream
- The benefits of implementing the value stream
- The Key Performance Indicators (KPIs)
- The purpose of the functional components
- The key data objects associated with the functional components

6.2 Objectives

The Strategy to Portfolio (S2P) Value Stream is focused on planning and choosing the right set of investments that IT should be making in any given period to respond to the demands placed upon it.

(Syllabus Reference: Unit 5, Strategy to Portfolio Value Stream, Learning Outcome 1: You should be able to describe the objectives of the Strategy to Portfolio (S2P) value stream.)

The objectives of the S2P Value Stream are as follows:
- To contribute to business strategy and planning enabling IT alignment with business plans
- To create an IT portfolio framework that allows IT organizations to optimize services provided to business by bringing together multiple functional areas
- To provide holistic views of IT portfolio activities through data integrations within multiple areas of the IT portfolio

6.3 Benefits

(Syllabus Reference: Unit 5, Strategy to Portfolio Value Stream, Learning Outcome 2: You should be able to explain the benefits of implementing the S2P Value Stream for the business.)

Most IT organizations already have IT portfolio processes and solutions in place, but suffer from the following limitations:
- Poor data consistency and quality
- No holistic IT portfolio view across the IT PMO and the Enterprise Architecture and Service Portfolio functional components
- Inconsistent Service and IT Portfolio Management processes
- Poor tracking and correlation of service lifecycle across conceptual, logical, and physical domains

The S2P Value Stream provides a blueprint for optimizing service and investment IT Portfolio Management. The end-to-end IT portfolio view provided by the S2P Value Stream raises the visibility of key data objects that are often overlooked during IT portfolio planning activities. Defining key data objects and relationships between data objects is easier when a proper framework is used.

The benefits of adopting the S2P Value Stream are:
- Holistic IT portfolio view across the IT PMO and the Enterprise Architecture and Service Portfolio functional components
- IT portfolio decisions based on business priorities
- Accurate visibility of business and IT demand
- IT portfolio data consistency
- Service lifecycle tracking through conceptual, logical, and physical domains
- Prioritized IT investment based on all IT portfolio facets including cost/value analysis, impacts on architecture, service roadmap, business priorities, etc.
- Re-balance IT investments between strategic and operational demand
- Solid communication with business stakeholders through roadmaps

6.4 Key Performance Indicators

(Syllabus Reference: Unit 5, Strategy to Portfolio Value Stream, Learning Outcome 3: You should be able to list the KPIs.)

- Business and IT alignment:
  - Ratio of new *versus* maintenance service
- Accurate visibility into demands from the business:
  - Demand requests, types, and delivery per service percentage of overall IT budget
- Service portfolio rationalization:
  - A formal Service Portfolio functional component process exists under the ownership of the Service Portfolio Management process owner
  - Taxonomies for understanding functional and technical redundancy and business value of the IT service are implemented
  - Processes for consistently evaluating and tagging portfolio entries are implemented
  - Service portfolio is subject to ongoing rationalization using the taxonomies, implemented as continuous improvement
  - Service and IT Portfolio Management are themselves rationalized with clear scoping and relationships established
- Service portfolio financial analysis:
  - Accounting records are produced on a regular basis to show the ongoing "investment & spend" in each service/application; these are compared with business outcomes and financial objectives that have been achieved
- Service portfolio reporting and analysis:
  - A service portfolio exists and is used as the basis for deciding which services to offer
- Service investment tracking:
  - The investment in each service is quantified in the service portfolio
  - Investment in each service is reported, starting with the initial investment, and followed by monthly, quarterly, or annual reporting of the ongoing budget spend (TCO)
- Improve customer satisfaction:
  - Satisfied customers per service/application
- Stewardship of IT investment:
  - CapEx *versus* OpEx
  - Software license percentage in use
  - Planned *versus* actual service costs
  - Average cost of IT delivery (per service/application) per customer

- Enterprise security alignment:
  - Frequency of security assessments against latest standards and guidelines
  - Noted deficiencies against security standards and policies

6.5 Functional Components

The Strategy to Portfolio Value Stream is the smallest value stream in terms of how many functional components and data objects it manages.

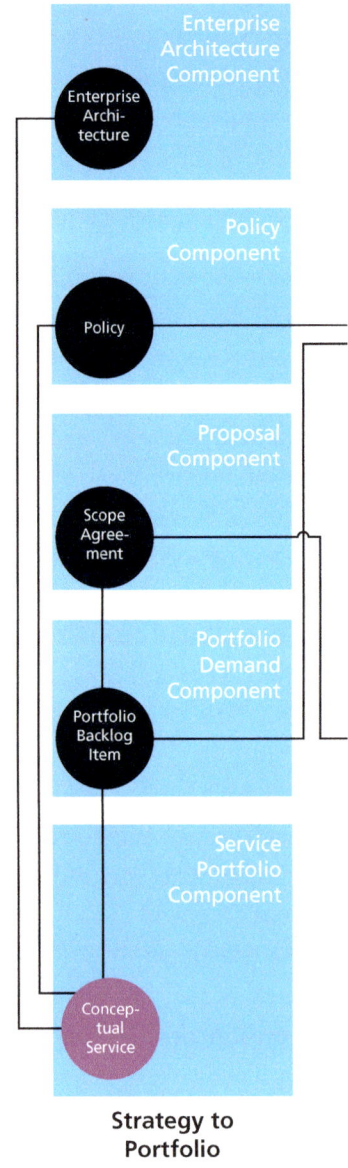

Figure 22: S2P Functional Components and Data Objects (Level 1)

The key functional components are as follows:
- Enterprise Architecture
- Policy
- Proposal
- Portfolio Demand
- Service Portfolio

The IT Investment Portfolio auxiliary functional component is associated with this value stream.

> See Appendix D for a summary of the functional components and the data objects in the Strategy to Portfolio Value Stream.

6.5.1 Enterprise Architecture Functional Component

(Syllabus Reference: Unit 5, Strategy to Portfolio Value Stream, Learning Outcome 4: You should be able to explain the purpose of the Enterprise Architecture functional component.)

The Enterprise Architecture functional component creates and manages long-term IT investment and the execution plan-of-action that are critical to business strategic objectives.

(Syllabus Reference: Unit 5, Strategy to Portfolio Value Stream, Learning Outcome 5: You should be able to briefly describe the data object(s) associated with the Enterprise Architecture functional component.)

The Enterprise Architecture data object includes references to collateral in the target state architecture landscape representing planned and deployed IT services.

6.5.2 Policy Functional Component

(Syllabus Reference: Unit 5, Strategy to Portfolio Value Stream, Learning Outcome 6: You should be able to explain the purpose of the Policy functional component.)

The Policy functional component manages creation, review, approval, and audit of all IT policies.

(Syllabus Reference: Unit 5, Strategy to Portfolio Value Stream, Learning Outcome 7: You should be able to briefly describe the data object(s) associated with the Policy functional component.)

The Policy data object can be thought as a central repository for storing and organizing all types of IT policies based on various templates and classification criteria; for example, acceptance criteria, exception processing, review periods, etc.

6.5.3 Proposal Functional Component

(Syllabus Reference: Unit 5, Strategy to Portfolio Value Stream, Learning Outcome 8: You should be able to explain the purpose of the Proposal functional component.)

The Proposal functional component manages the portfolio of IT proposals that are proposed, approved, active, deferred, or rejected.

(Syllabus Reference: Unit 5, Strategy to Portfolio Value Stream, Learning Outcome 9: You should be able to briefly describe the data object(s) associated with the Proposal functional component.)

The Scope Agreement data object is the authoritative source for the list of all IT proposals requested over a given time period. This data object is used for building the IT investment plan of record for the company or a specific line of business or function. Scope Agreements reflect budget, costs/benefit projections, scope, status, and other key attributes of the work, such as when is it needed, who might deliver it, etc. Views can be created for specific stakeholders, such as line of business, or holistically, such as company-wide.

6.5.4 Portfolio Demand Functional Component

(Syllabus Reference: Unit 5, Strategy to Portfolio Value Stream, Learning Outcome 10: You should be able to explain the purpose of the Portfolio Demand functional component.)

The Portfolio Demand functional component logs, maintains, and evaluates all demands (new service, enhancements, defects) coming into IT through a single funnel, correlating incoming demand to similar existing demand or creating new demand.

The "single funnel" may be a virtual concept encompassing project ideation, service request management, incident management, continuous improvement, and other well-known demand channels.

(Syllabus Reference: Unit 5, Strategy to Portfolio Value Stream, Learning Outcome 11: You should be able to briefly describe the data object(s) associated with the Portfolio Demand functional component.)

The Portfolio Backlog Item data object represents what the demand entails; for example, who wants it, why they want it, etc. Together, the set of Portfolio Backlog Items represents the repository of all incoming demands; this includes but is not limited to new requests, enhancement requests, and defect fix requests.

6.5.5 Service Portfolio Functional Component

(Syllabus Reference: Unit 5, Strategy to Portfolio Value Stream, Learning Outcome 12: You should be able to explain the purpose of the Service Portfolio functional component.)

The purpose of the Service Portfolio functional component is to manage the portfolio of services in plan, transition, production, and retirement. It is the authoritative source for the list of services that IT delivers, has delivered in the past, or brokers to itself and the business. Any IT service within the Service Portfolio functional component often corresponds to one or more entries in the Offer Catalog.

(Syllabus Reference: Unit 5, Strategy to Portfolio Value Stream, Learning Outcome 13: You should be able to briefly describe the data object(s) associated with the Service Portfolio functional component.)

The Conceptual Service data object represents the business perspective of the service and is the service interaction or the business capability of the service. It is the level suitable for discussing aspects that characterize the service as the product of IT activity including business value, investment history and outlook, value earned, and return on investment. It is described in terms that are understood by CxO-level persons who decide on the assignment of budget and resources in order to build and maintain the service.

The Conceptual Service Blueprint auxiliary data object provides service process and delivery visualization from the customer's point of view for a given Conceptual Service.

6.5.6 IT Investment Portfolio Auxiliary Functional Component

(Syllabus Reference: Unit 5, Strategy to Portfolio Value Stream, Learning Outcome 14: You should be able to explain the purpose of the IT Investment Portfolio auxiliary functional component.)

The IT Investment Portfolio auxiliary functional component is auxiliary to the S2P Value Stream and is primary in the IT Financial Management guidance document. The purpose of the IT Investment Portfolio auxiliary functional component is to manage the portfolio of all authorized IT investments.

(Syllabus Reference: Unit 5, Strategy to Portfolio Value Stream, Learning Outcome 15: You should be able to briefly describe the data object(s) associated with the IT Investment Portfolio auxiliary functional component.)

The IT Budget Item data object is an authoritative list of the approved IT investment pertaining to a service. This set of records will help to identify approved budget over different time periods; by financial year, by Conceptual Service, for example.

6.6 Summary

The purpose of the Strategy to Portfolio Value Stream is to manage your portfolio and investments to drive business innovation.

- It provides the strategy to balance and broker your portfolio
- It provides a unified viewpoint across the PMO, Enterprise Architecture, and Service Portfolio
- It improves data quality to support decision-making

- It provides KPIs and develops roadmaps to improve business communication

6.7 Recommended Reading

The following are recommended sources of further information for this chapter:
- The IT4IT Reference Architecture, Version 2.1, Chapter 5

6.8 Exercise 5: Strategy to Portfolio Value Stream

1. What are the objectives of the S2P Value Stream?
   _____
   _____

2. What are the benefits of implementing the S2P Value Stream?
   _____
   _____

3. What are three KPIs for the S2P Value Stream?
   _____
   _____

4. Complete the first column in the following table, by entering the relevant number(s) to identify the description matching the functional component.

Answer	Functional Component	Description
_____	Enterprise Architecture	1. Logs, maintains, and evaluates all demands (new service, enhancements, defects) coming into IT through a single funnel. Correlates incoming demand to similar existing demand or creates new demand.
_____	Portfolio Demand	2. Manages the portfolio of IT proposals that are proposed, approved, active, deferred, or rejected.
_____	Service Portfolio	3. Manages the creation, review, approval, and audit of all IT policies.

Answer	Functional Component	Description
_____	Proposal	4. Manages the entire portfolio of services in plan, transition, production, and retirement.
_____	Policy	5. Creates and manages long-term IT investment and execution plan-of-action that are critical to business strategic objectives.

5. Complete the first column in the following table, by entering the relevant number(s) to identify the data object associated with the functional component.

Answer	Data Object	Functional Component
_____	Portfolio Backlog Item	1. Policy
_____	Conceptual Service	2. Proposal
_____	Enterprise Architecture	3. Portfolio Demand
_____	Scope Agreement	4. Enterprise Architecture
_____	Policy	5. Service Portfolio

6.9 Test Yourself Questions

Q1: Which of the following is an objective of the Strategy to Portfolio Value Stream?
   A. Creating a framework for managing Subscriptions and total cost of service
   B. Enabling IT alignment with business plans
   C. Integrating the work of IT operations to enhance services and efficiencies
   D. Making service delivery predictable

Q2: Which of the following is a benefit of implementing the S2P Value Stream?
   A. Accurate visibility of business and IT demand
   B. Control points in place to manage quality and cost of services
   C. Increased rate of first call resolution
   D. Providing visibility across service Subscription, Usage, and Chargeback

Q3: Which of the following is a KPI for business and IT alignment in the S2P Value Stream?
A. The average cost of IT delivery per service per customer
B. The planned *versus* actual service costs
C. The ratio of new *versus* maintenance services
D. The service portfolio is used as the basis of deciding which services to offer

Q4: Which of the following describes the purpose of the Portfolio Demand functional component?
A. Manages the creation, review, approval, and audit of all IT policies
B. Logs, maintains, and evaluates all demands coming into IT through a single funnel
C. Presents consumable Offers derived from Service Catalog Entries with associated descriptions
D. Provides a modern IT engagement/consumption experience, enabling users to acquire services

Q5: Which functional component within the S2P Value Stream manages the portfolio of IT proposals that are proposed, approved, active, deferred, or rejected?
A. Policy
B. Portfolio
C. Project
D. Proposal

Q6: Complete the sentence: The _____ data object associated with the _____ functional component reflects key attributes of proposed work created from rationalized Portfolio Backlog Items.
A. Conceptual Service Blueprint, Portfolio Demand
B. Conceptual Service, Project
C. Enterprise Architecture, Policy
D. Scope Agreement, Proposal

Q7: Which data object associated with the Enterprise Architecture functional component includes references to collateral representing planned and deployed IT services?
A. Conceptual Service
B. Enterprise Architecture
C. Logical Service
D. Service Design

Q8: What data object associated with the Service Portfolio functional component represents the business perspective of the service?
A. Conceptual Service
B. IT Initiative
C. Portfolio Backlog Item
D. Service Release

Chapter 7

The Requirement to Deploy Value Stream

7.1 Key Learning Points

This chapter will help you understand the Requirement to Deploy Value Stream.

Key Points Explained

This chapter will help you to understand and explain:
- The objectives of the value stream
- The benefits of implementing the value stream
- The Key Performance Indicators (KPIs)
- The purpose of the functional components
- The key data objects associated with the functional components

7.2 Objectives

The Requirement to Deploy (R2D) Value Stream is focused on building or sourcing services, turning the investment decisions from the S2P Value Stream into services, planning the work, designing or developing the service, testing the service, and releasing the service.

(Syllabus Reference: Unit 6, Requirement to Deploy Value Stream, Learning Outcome 1: You should be able to describe the objectives of the Requirement to Deploy (R2D) Value Stream.)

The objectives for the R2D Value Stream are as follows:
- To make service delivery predictable: even across geographically dispersed teams, multiple suppliers, and multiple development methodologies
- To ensure that each Service Release is high quality, fit-for-purpose, and meets customer expectations
- To understand the evolving relationship between planning and building
- To standardize service development and delivery to the point where re-use of service components is the norm

- To build a culture of collaboration between IT operations and IT development to support Service Release success
- To put rigorous information management controls in place to lessen the impact of high staff turnover
- To enable more predictable outcomes without driving out innovation

7.3 Benefits

(Syllabus Reference: Unit 6, Requirement to Deploy Value Stream, Learning Outcome 2: You should be able to explain the benefits of implementing the R2D Value Stream for the business.)

The benefits of implementing the R2D Value Stream are as follows:
- A maximized pipeline of projects and smaller grained demand requests leads to faster time-to-market in service realization
- Predictable outcomes ensure that the delivered application or service performs are as requested, leading to higher rates of user acceptance and better business alignment
- Established control points to manage the quality, utility, security, and cost of services, independent of development method or delivery source
- Increased management information for traceability and benchmarking of internal and external service developers and suppliers
- Assurance that all services are designed in accordance with standards and policies
- Improved inputs to IT Financial Management on service cost
- Assurance that applications and services are related to business value by creating and maintaining the service blueprint
- Accelerated sourcing and delivery of applications and services through best practices, such as re-use, automation, and collaboration

7.4 Key Performance Indicators

(Syllabus Reference: Unit 6, Requirement to Deploy Value Stream, Learning Outcome 3: You should be able to list the KPIs.)

- Improve quality:
  - Number of escaped defects (defects found by customers)
  - % of actual *versus* planned executed tests

- % of critical defects found early in unit testing *versus* User Acceptance Testing (UAT)
- Improve project and feature execution:
  - % of projects (project tasks, stories, other demand requests) on time
  - % of healthy projects (projects without unresolved urgent issues)
  - Deviation of planned to actual work hours
  - Number of identified issues
  - Number of opened risks
  - Amount of backlog/work-in-process
  - Arrival and departure rate for work
- Improve stewardship of IT investment:
  - % of actual *versus* planned project cost
  - % of change in project cost
  - % of budget at risk
- Increase automation adoption:
  - % of automated tests
- Achieve development process excellence:
  - % of requirements tested, authorized, completed
  - % of requirements traced to tests
  - % of reviewed requirements
  - % of successful builds
  - % of changes resulting in Incidents
  - Ratio of detected to closed defects at release
- Improve early life success of releases:
  - % of Incidents during warranty period
  - % of successful/unsuccessful deployments for the project
  - % of emergency changes
  - Pass rates on UAT/validated requirements
- Operations and development collaboration:
  - Trend on early life support/UAT success metrics
  - % rework
- Improve financial visibility:
  - Planned cost *versus* actual cost
- Maintain a linkage between business services and IT Initiatives:
  - Aggregate (roll up) service development costs by business service
- High quality service design specifications at the outset:
  - % reduction in the rework required for new or changed service solutions in subsequent lifecycle stages

- Integration test success:
  - Trend on the number of installation errors in all the packages in the integration environment
  - Number of applications or services that require exceptions outside the existing infrastructure portfolio
- Design-review to ensure application design complies with all policies, including security:
  - Number of application designs that pass a security policy review
- Early testing of applications for security vulnerabilities:
  - % of high severity security defects fixed before application is released

7.5 Functional Components

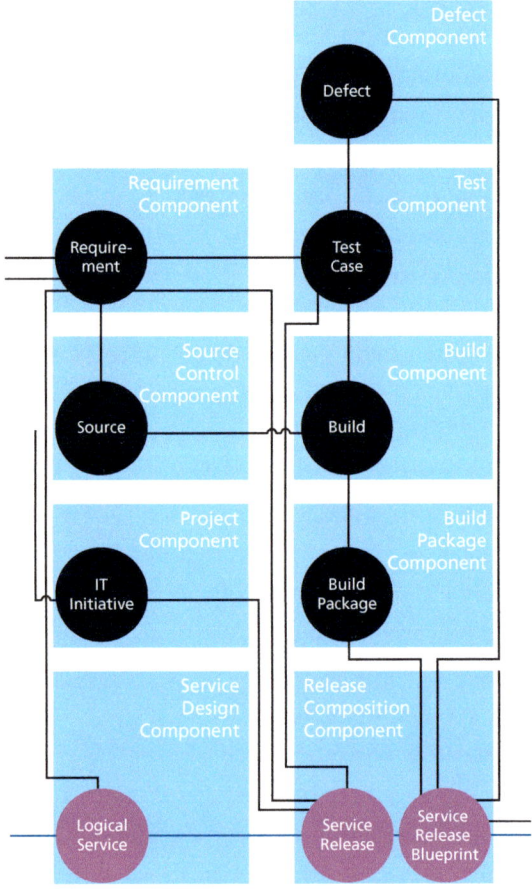

Figure 23:   R2D Functional Components and Data Objects (Level 1)

The key functional components are as follows:
- Project
- Requirement
- Service Design
- Source Control
- Build
- Build Package
- Release Composition
- Test
- Defect

> See Appendix D for a summary of the functional components and the data objects in the Requirement to Deploy Value Stream.

7.5.1 Project Functional Component
(Syllabus Reference: Unit 6, Requirement to Deploy Value Stream, Learning Outcome 4: You should be able to explain the purpose of the Project functional component.)

The Project functional component coordinates the creation and provides ongoing execution oversight of IT Initiatives aimed at the development of new services, or enhancements to existing services. The IT Initiatives are based on the specifications outlined in the Scope Agreement, and include cost, time, scope, and quality.

The Project functional component:
- Governs, coordinates, influences, and directs initiative execution
- Maintains the connection between initiatives, associated applications, and service(s) being developed
- Aggregates, tracks, and reports status (such as resources consumed against project plan, or project burn down)
- Ensures that financial goals and boundary conditions are adhered to, and coordinates the acquisition of resources (such as hardware, software, and people) required to source/create a service in a particular project

(Syllabus Reference: Unit 6, Requirement to Deploy Value Stream, Learning Outcome 5: You should be able to briefly describe the data object(s) associated with the Project functional component.)

The IT Initiative data object details the scope of the work to be performed and created from and associated with the Scope Agreement.

7.5.2 Requirement Functional Component

(Syllabus Reference: Unit 6, Requirement to Deploy Value Stream, Learning Outcome 6: You should be able to explain the purpose of the Requirement functional component.)

The Requirement functional component:
- Manages Requirements through the lifecycle of a service
- Captures service-level requirements as Requirements
- Collects, refines, scopes, and tracks progress of Requirements even before and after an IT Initiative has concluded
- Maintains the traceability of each Requirement to the original source (demand, IT or business standard or policy, and/or requestor) and to the appropriate Source and/or Test Cases throughout the service lifecycle
- Derives product or program backlogs, which will ultimately serve as queues for enhancing IT services

(Syllabus Reference: Unit 6, Requirement to Deploy Value Stream, Learning Outcome 7: You should be able to briefly describe the data object(s) associated with the Requirement functional component.)

The Requirement data object records details of the needs or conditions to meet for a new or altered service.

7.5.3 Service Design Functional Component

(Syllabus Reference: Unit 6, Requirement to Deploy Value Stream, Learning Outcome 8: You should be able to explain the purpose of the Service Design functional component.)

The Service Design functional component:
- Identifies the new or existing services required to meet the needs of the Scope Agreement and IT Initiative, including both service systems and service offers

- Produces a Logical Service that describes the service structure and behavior considering both the service system and the service offer, based on the Conceptual Service and Portfolio Backlog Items (from the S2P Value Stream)
- Creates a service design specification document (Logical Service Blueprint) that is compliant with all standards and policies
- Ensures that the service is architected to meet the KPIs and SLAs
- Includes creation of various architectural artifacts (data flow diagrams, technical schematics, etc.) that comply with the IT Initiative specifications and boundaries
- Identifies the service delivery model (in-source, outsource, etc.), and the service suppliers to meet the requirements within the chosen delivery model
- Enables interaction with IT operations to develop support plan/requirements for an IT service; IT will put instrumentation in place so that IT can capture empirical data about how IT services are performing rather than relying only on anecdotal input from the user community

The output of the Service Design functional component is used by the Source data object to source, create, and secure the service. The traceability is done through the Requirement functional component.

(Syllabus Reference: Unit 6, Requirement to Deploy Value Stream, Learning Outcome 9: You should be able to briefly describe the data object(s) associated with the Service Design functional component.)

The Logical Service data object represents the bridge between the service interaction and service system. It is a user-friendly name of the service system and is meaningful to the service provider, but may not be known specifically to the business. It represents the grouping of logical components necessary to provide the expected outcome or service interaction.

7.5.4 Source Control Functional Component

(Syllabus Reference: Unit 6, Requirement to Deploy Value Stream, Learning Outcome 10: You should be able to explain the purpose of the Source Control functional component.)

The Source Control functional component:
- Manages the development of source code or infrastructure based on the Logical Service Blueprint, Service Design Package, and IT Initiative priorities
- Ensures that the source code meets the design specifications, organizational policies, standards, and non-functional requirements so that the service can be operated successfully and meets customer expectations
- Manages source code images and stores them in a Source data object repository
- Receives Defects and input from the Defect functional component to enable the development of fixes or documented workarounds; it manages the development backlog of Requirements and Defects in accordance with the Service Design Package and Service Release
- Includes the creation of automated test scripts including unit testing and scripts for static application security testing that follow a formal software security assurance methodology
  For existing services being changed, it includes the execution of security tests on core code to identify existing security issues at the start of the development cycle so that assessment of scope/requirements set/schedule can be negotiated early.

(Syllabus Reference: Unit 6, Requirement to Deploy Value Stream, Learning Outcome 11: You should be able to briefly describe the data object(s) associated with the Source Control functional component.)

The Source data object is the created or purchased solution to meet the requirements for a particular Service Release.

7.5.5 Build Functional Component

(Syllabus Reference: Unit 6, Requirement to Deploy Value Stream, Learning Outcome 12: You should be able to explain the purpose of the Build functional component.)

The Build functional component:
- Receives the Source data object from the Source Control functional component and manages the creation, implementation, automation, and security and storage of all Builds; it manages Builds and versioning in a Definitive Media Library (DML)

- Creates the Build from the Source data object for a particular service component
- Automates the Build process through automated Build storage procedures and automated compilation techniques and tools
- Monitors and reports on the results of each integration Build
- Initiates or automates the delivery of Builds to the Build Package functional component for validation by the acceptance testing team as candidate release builds
- Runs dynamic application security testing no later than when the final Build data object is received and before the RFCs are created for moving the new or changed service into production

(Syllabus Reference: Unit 6, Requirement to Deploy Value Stream, Learning Outcome 13: You should be able to briefly describe the data object(s) associated with the Build functional component.)

The Build data object is created from Source and versioned.

7.5.6 Build Package Functional Component
(Syllabus Reference: Unit 6, Requirement to Deploy Value Stream, Learning Outcome 14: You should be able to explain the purpose of the Build Package functional component.)

The Build Package functional component:
- Creates a deployable package made up of one or many Builds
- Manages the Build Packages and relationships to the Service Release Blueprints

(Syllabus Reference: Unit 6, Requirement to Deploy Value Stream, Learning Outcome 15: You should be able to briefly describe the data object(s) associated with the Build Package functional component.)

The Build Package data object is a compilation of one or many Builds in a deployable package.

7.5.7 Release Composition Functional Component

(Syllabus Reference: Unit 6, Requirement to Deploy Value Stream, Learning Outcome 16: You should be able to explain the purpose of the Release Composition functional component.)

The Release Composition functional component:
- Manages the Release Package, Service Release, Service Release Blueprints, and overall Service Release for developing and delivering new or changed services to the R2F Value Stream Fulfillment Execution functional component to facilitate a smooth transition to IT operations
- Creates the Service Release, Service Release Blueprint, and Release Packages that will be utilized by the Test functional component and later the Fulfillment Execution functional component (R2F Value Stream) to create a specific deployment for a specific IT service instance (including service system and/or service offer)
- Manages the release artifacts within the Release Package by centralizing all elements of the Service Release Blueprint from the various functional components, and begins the creation of monitors, batch processing, backup/restore, etc. for the service, to ensure supportability as part of IT operations enablement
  These release artifacts include:
    - Requirement functional component: Requirements per Release Package
    - Source Control functional component, as well as maintenance scripts: documentation
    - Build Package functional component: Build Package
    - Test functional component: test results as well as automated tests for validation post deployment
    - Defect functional component: Known Errors (issues/defects)

(Syllabus Reference: Unit 6, Requirement to Deploy Value Stream, Learning Outcome 17: You should be able to briefly describe the data object(s) associated with the Release Composition functional component.)

The Service Release data object represents a planned release of a version of the service system.

The Service Release Blueprint data object provides the planned design/configuration of the components of the service system.

7.5.8 Test Functional Component

(Syllabus Reference: Unit 6, Requirement to Deploy Value Stream, Learning Outcome 18: You should be able to explain the purpose of the Test functional component.)

The Test functional component:
- Plans and executes tests to ensure the IT service will support the customer's requirements at the agreed service levels
- Prepares the test environment, plans and designs tests, and executes all functional and non-functional tests, including usability, security testing, performance, and stress testing
- Creates Defect data objects that are consumed by the Defect functional component
- Provides test execution reports for the tested Requirements, and ensures that the operations tooling works as expected (monitors, etc.); it also manages test data, test automation, and test scripts where appropriate

(Syllabus Reference: Unit 6, Requirement to Deploy Value Stream, Learning Outcome 19: You should be able to briefly describe the data object(s) associated with the Test functional component.)

The Test Case data object is used to validate that the Service Release is fit-for-purpose.

7.5.9 Defect Functional Component

(Syllabus Reference: Unit 6, Requirement to Deploy Value Stream, Learning Outcome 20: You should be able to explain the purpose of the Defect functional component.)

The Defect functional component:
- Keeps track of all Defects by registering Defects of all types (including security-related Defects)
- Analyzes Defects, finds resolutions, and associates Defects with Requirements and Known Errors
- Consumes Defects from both the D2C Value Stream Problem functional component and the Test functional component that are in turn consumed by the Source Control functional component for review and resolution

- Documents issues that should be communicated to the Release Composition functional component
- Decides on the target release and report Defect status; it also converts unresolved Defects to Known Errors for Problem Management (in the D2C Value Stream)

(Syllabus Reference: Unit 6, Requirement to Deploy Value Stream, Learning Outcome 21: You should be able to briefly describe the data object(s) associated with the Defect functional component.)

The Defect data object is an issue with the Service Release Blueprint which should be remediated to fulfill the associated Requirements.

7.6 Summary

The purpose of the Requirement to Deploy Value Stream is to prioritize every requirement to build the best services and deploy them
- It provides a framework for creating, modifying, or sourcing a service
- It supports agile and traditional development methodologies
- It enables visibility of the quality, utility, schedule, and cost of services you deliver
- It defines continuous integration and deployment control points

7.7 Recommended Reading

The following are recommended sources of further information for this chapter:
- The IT4IT Reference Architecture, Version 2.1, Chapter 6

7.8 Exercise 6: Requirement to Deploy Value Stream

1. What are the objectives of the R2D Value Stream?
   _____
   _____

2. What are the benefits of implementing the R2D Value Stream?
   _____
   _____

Ch. 7 THE REQUIREMENT TO DEPLOY VALUE STREAM

3. What are three KPIs for the R2D Value Stream?

   _____

   _____

4. Complete the first column in the following table, by entering the relevant number(s) to identify the description matching the functional component.

Answer	Functional Component	Description
_____	Build	1. Plan, store, and execute tests that ensure that the IT service will support the customer's requirements.
_____	Build Package	2. Manages the Release Package, Service Release, Service Release Blueprints, and overall Service Release for developing and delivering new or changed services.
_____	Defect	3. Ensures that the source is developed in accordance with design specifications, policies, standards, and non-functional requirements.
_____	Project	4. Produces a Logical Service, which describes the service structure and behavior considering both the service system and the service offer.
_____	Release Composition	5. Creates a deployable package made up of one or many Builds.
_____	Requirement	6. Provides ongoing execution oversight of IT Initiatives aimed at the creation of new or enhancements to existing services.
_____	Service Design	7. Manages Requirements through the lifecycle of a service.
_____	Source Control	8. Manages the creation, implementation, automation, security, and storage of all Builds.
_____	Test	9. Manages Defects, keeping track of their status, and their relationships back to Requirements and Known Errors.

5. Complete the first column in the following table, by entering the relevant number(s) to identify the data object associated with the functional component.

Answer	Data Object	Functional Component
	Logical Service	1. Requirement
	Build	2. Source Control
	Service Release Blueprint	3. Project
	Requirement	4. Build Package
	Defect	5. Release Composition
	Test Case	6. Service Design
	Build Package	7. Test
	Source	8. Build
	IT Initiative	9. Defect

7.9 Test Yourself Questions

Q1: Which of the following is an objective of the Requirement to Deploy Value Stream?
  A. Creating a consumption experience that consumers recognize and value
  B. Enabling a unified viewpoint across multiple areas of the IT portfolio
  C. Ensuring that each Service Release is high quality and fit-for-purpose
  D. Providing a comprehensive overview of IT operations and services

Q2: Which of the following is a benefit of implementing the R2D Value Stream?
  A. Accurate visibility of business and IT demand
  B. Ensuring that all services are designed in accordance with standards and policies
  C. Providing visibility across service Subscription, Usage, and Chargeback
  D. Service lifecycle tracking through conceptual, logical, and physical domains

Q3: Which of the following is a KPI in the R2D Value Stream for improving the stewardship of IT investment?
   A. Completed service requests
   B. Costs per service and per fulfillment step
   C. Number of purchase orders per time period
   D. Percentage of actual *versus* planned project cost

Q4: Which of the following describes the purpose of the Service Design functional component?
   A. Ensures that the service is developed in accordance with design specifications, standards, and non-functional requirements
   B. Manages the entire portfolio of services in plan, transition, production, and retirement
   C. Manages the Release Package, Service Release, Service Release Blueprints, and overall Service Release for developing and delivering new or changed services
   D. Produces a Logical Service, which describes the service structure and behavior considering both the service system and the service offer

Q5: Which functional component within the R2D Value Stream provides oversight of IT Initiatives aimed at the creation of new or enhanced services?
   A. Build
   B. Fulfillment Execution
   C. Project
   D. Release Composition

Q6: Complete the sentence: The _____ data object associated with the _____ functional component represents a planned release of a version of the service system.
   A. Build, Build Package
   B. Fulfillment Request, Service Fulfillment
   C. Request, Request Rationalization
   D. Service Release, Release Composition

Q7: What data object associated with the Source Control functional component represents the created or purchased solution?
A. Build Package
B. Service Release
C. Source
D. Target Solution

Q8: What data object details the scope of work to be performed and created from and associated with the Scope Agreement?
A. Incident
B. IT Initiative
C. Portfolio Backlog Item
D. Requirement

Chapter 8

The Request to Fulfill Value Stream

8.1 Key Learning Points
This chapter will help you understand the Request to Fulfill Value Stream.

Key Points Explained
This chapter will help you to understand and explain:
- The objectives of the value stream
- The benefits of implementing the value stream
- The Key Performance Indicators (KPIs)
- The purpose of the functional components
- The key data objects associated with the functional components

8.2 Objectives
(Syllabus Reference: Unit 7, Request to Fulfill Value Stream, Learning Outcome 1: You should be able to describe objectives of the Request to Fulfill (R2F) Value Stream.)

The objectives for the R2F Value Stream are as follows:
- To provide a blueprint for creating a streamlined consumption experience that will consistently engage consumers and eliminate the need for them to avoid working with their IT organization

This is achieved by:
- The ability to package deliverables as offers that consumers recognize and value, abstracting away confusing technology choices and complex fulfillment processes
- The ability to present and manage an inviting consumption experience that exposes a variety of opportunities to acquire services, goods, knowledge, and/or support

8.3 Benefits

(Syllabus Reference: Unit 7, Request to Fulfill Value Stream, Learning Outcome 2: You should be able to explain the benefits of implementing the R2F Value Stream for the business.)

The benefits of implementing the R2F Value Stream are:
- Provision of a blueprint for increasing business innovation velocity through the facilitation of a service consumption experience which allows consumers to easily find and subscribe to goods and services through a self-service engagement model
- Provision of a functional framework that delineates between a single Offer Catalog and multiple Catalog Compositions to reduce complexity in the IT shopping experience
- Provision of an architectural foundation for moving from traditional IT request management to service brokerage that increases both business and IT effectiveness
- Increased fulfillment efficiency and consistency through standard change deployment and automation
- Holistic visibility and traceability across service Subscription, Usage, and Chargeback to improve IT Financial Management
- Increased cost optimization; for example, by canceling expired Subscriptions and reclaiming resources, such as unused Subscriptions, and/or Licenses

8.4 Key Performance Indicators

(Syllabus Reference: Unit 7, Request to Fulfill Value Stream, Learning Outcome 3: You should be able to list the KPIs.)
- Ability to meet customer expectations:
  - New or modified Subscriptions per time period
  - % and number of Subscription requests complying with or breaching SLAs or OLAs
  - Number of Subscription requests accepted and rejected by the requestor for the first time right delivery/fulfillment
  - Variation in the average time to fulfill Subscription requests for the predictability of delivery
  - Number of Incidents related to request fulfillment
  - Arrival and departure rate of service requests

- Reduce costs:
  - Costs (burned resources) per service and per fulfillment step
  - Breakdown of self-source fulfillments *versus* one-off fulfillments
  - % and number of fulfillments requiring human intervention to be completed
  - Number of service request queues being managed
- External service provider compliance:
  - Number of purchase orders per time period
  - % and number of orders delivered and accepted complying with underpinning contract agreements
  - % and number of delivered orders breaching underpinning contract agreements
  - Number of Incidents related to purchase order fulfillment
  - Number of purchase orders unfulfilled at the end of a given period
  - Number of orders delivered and accepted by the requestor per time period
  - Number of purchase orders rejected via no delivery or cancelled purchase orders
- Increase speed/agility/flexibility (operational performance):
  - Completed service requests
  - Service request work-in-progress
  - Number of interactions with consumers per service during delivery
  - % of work-in-progress within SLA
  - % of completed work within SLA

8.5 Functional Components

(Syllabus Reference: Unit 7, Request to Fulfill Value Stream, Learning Outcome 4: You should be able to explain the purpose of primary and secondary functional components within the R2F Value Stream.)

The Request to Fulfill (R2F) Value Stream contains primary and secondary functional components. Primary functional components are core to the value stream and are essential for managing the service at this stage of its lifecycle. Secondary functional components are not dedicated to the R2F Value Stream but provide relevant data objects to primary functional components.

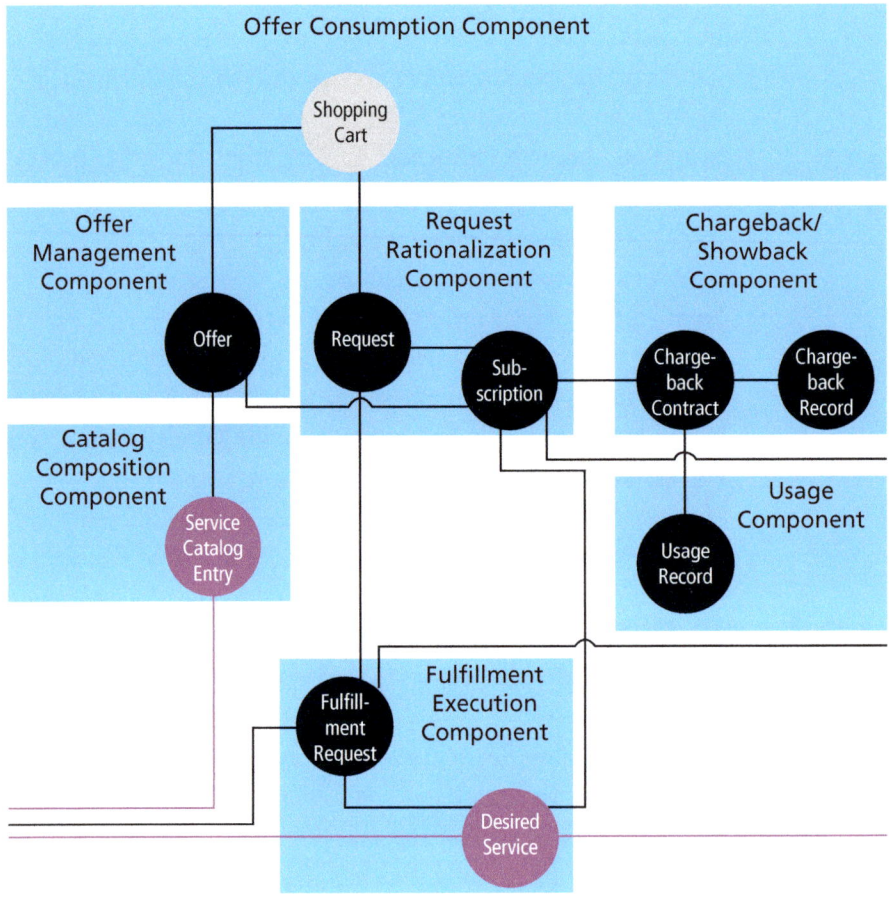

Request to Fulfill

Figure 24: R2F Functional Components and Data Objects (Level 1)

The key functional components are:
- Engagement Experience Portal (secondary functional component)
- Offer Consumption
- Offer Management
- Catalog Composition
- Request Rationalization
- Fulfillment Execution
- Usage
- Chargeback/Showback
- Knowledge & Collaboration (supporting function)

See Appendix D for a summary of the functional components and the data objects in the Request to Fulfill Value Stream.

Request to Fulfill is a continuous cycle as shown in Figure 25. The cycle is as follows:
1. Maintain catalog items (including those sourced from external vendors)
2. Create consolidated offerings from the available services in the catalog
3. Order service from the web shop
4. Manage the request, approval, and monitor fulfillment; manage the Subscriptions
5. Deploy, release, and/or provisioning, including updating the CMDB and license administration
6. Monitor actual usage and consumption
7. Show actual cost and consumption to user and/or service owner
8. Cancel or modify Subscription

8.5.1 Engagement Experience Portal Secondary Functional Component

The Engagement Experience Portal secondary functional component is based on a system of engagement design pattern where consumers access different functional components through a common user experience.

(Syllabus Reference: Unit 7, Request to Fulfill Value Stream, Learning Outcome 5: You should be able to explain the objectives of the Engagement Experience Portal secondary functional component.)

The objectives of the Engagement Experience Portal are to:
- Drive the consumption through the Offer Catalog
- Enable collaboration between communities of interest
- Obtain support through a self-service interface
- Access knowledge that enables them to be better informed about services offered by IT

(Syllabus Reference: Unit 7, Request to Fulfill Value Stream, Learning Outcome 6: You should be able to explain the purpose of the Engagement Experience Portal secondary functional component.)

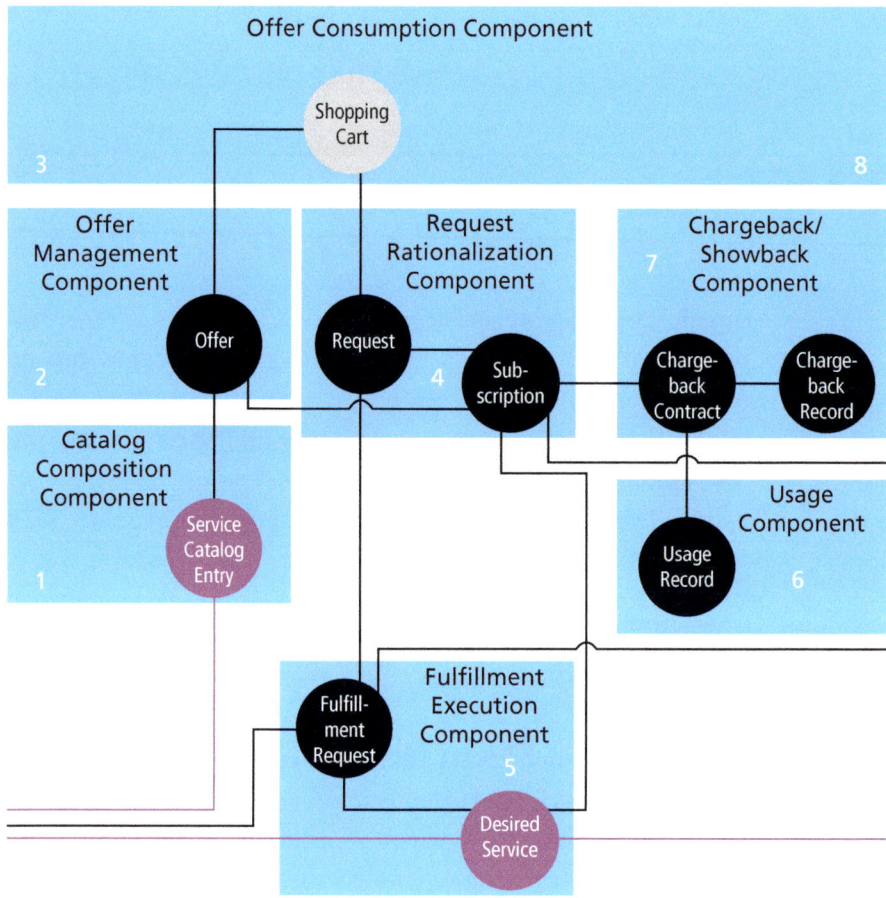

Request to Fulfill

Figure 25: R2F Cycle View

The Engagement Experience Portal secondary functional component:
- Facilitates service consumption by connecting potential consumers with the right information, goods, services, or capability at the right time through a single experience, taking into account the consumer profile
- Provides an intuitive experience that draws consumers in rather than being viewed as an inhibitor to productivity that is forced upon them
- Provides the consumer with a self-configurable experience, and interface supported across multiple devices
- Provides plug-and-play connectivity for components that need to be exposed through the portal

(Syllabus Reference: Unit 7, Request to Fulfill Value Stream, Learning Outcome 7: You should be able to briefly describe the data object(s) associated with the Engagement Experience Portal secondary functional component.)

The User Profile data object contains personal data associated with a specific user and the explicit digital representation of a person's identity.

8.5.2 Offer Consumption Functional Component

(Syllabus Reference: Unit 7, Request to Fulfill Value Stream, Learning Outcome 8: You should be able to explain the purpose of the Offer Consumption functional component.)

The Offer Consumption functional component:
- Presents consumable Offers derived from Service Catalog Entries with associated descriptions, pictures, prices, and purchasing options to prospective consumers
- Facilitates consumption/management of and payment for IT services rendered
- Enables consumers to manage their Subscriptions and present a personalized experience, which includes consumer-specific information such as personal preferences, location, or job function; this includes:
    - Viewing Subscription/service status, costs, usage, etc.
    - Adding new Subscriptions, ordering new services, or service instances
    - Modifying Subscription parameters (also known as upgrading/downgrading)
    - Cancelling/ending service Subscriptions

(Syllabus Reference: Unit 7, Request to Fulfill Value Stream, Learning Outcome 9: You should be able to briefly describe the data object(s) associated with the Offer Consumption functional component.)

The Shopping Cart data object contains the IT services that the user wants to order; the object only exists during the actual shopping session.

8.5.3 Offer Management Functional Component

Offers are based on Service Catalog Entries developed in the Catalog Composition functional component; they are created from the consumer point of view and can be tailored to different personas, roles, or functions using profiling.

(Syllabus Reference: Unit 7, Request to Fulfill Value Stream, Learning Outcome 10: You should be able to explain the purpose of the Offer Management functional component.)

The Offer Management functional component:
- Aggregates all Catalog Composition items and external supplier catalogs into consumable Offers that users can order through the Offer Consumption functional component
- Builds and publishes the various offerings into Offer Catalogs for various populations; this enables Offers to be grouped into an Offer Catalog to expose them as a collection of consumable items for a given group of consumers
- Fulfills each Offer through numerous underlying Catalog Compositions

(Syllabus Reference: Unit 7, Request to Fulfill Value Stream, Learning Outcome 11: You should be able to briefly describe the data object(s) associated with the Offer Management functional component.)

The Offer data object defines how a Service Catalog Entry will be instantiated and under what terms and conditions – price, deployment, approval, workflow, service level (contract), etc.

The Offer Catalog auxiliary data object is a set or collection of Offers that are grouped together as something that can be consumed by certain consumers or consumer groups.

8.5.4 Catalog Composition Functional Component

(Syllabus Reference: Unit 7, Request to Fulfill Value Stream, Learning Outcome 12: You should be able to explain the purpose of the Catalog Composition functional component.)

The Catalog Composition functional component creates, updates, and publishes Service Catalog Entries including all their dependencies necessary to be presented as an Offer in the Offer Management functional component.

(Syllabus Reference: Unit 7, Request to Fulfill Value Stream, Learning Outcome 13: You should be able to briefly describe the data object(s) associated with the Catalog Composition functional component.)

The Service Catalog Entry data object is an authoritative source for the consolidated set of technical capabilities and specific options available from a service system, which can be delivered by the service provider. It serves as the bridge between the service system and the service offer.

Service Catalog Entries are created from the Service Release Blueprint in the Release Composition functional component (R2D Value Stream). Service Catalog Entries are created and updated to prepare them for consumption, including configurable options (e.g., pricing, subscription terms, bundles, service level, support conditions, etc.).

8.5.5 Request Rationalization Functional Component

(Syllabus Reference: Unit 7, Request to Fulfill Value Stream, Learning Outcome 14: You should be able to explain the purpose of the Request Rationalization functional component.)

The Request Rationalization functional component:
- Rationalizes, breaks down, and routes "clean order" requests (ready for fulfillment) to appropriate Fulfillment Execution engines or providers in order to deliver services to consumers; this may involve breaking down a single order/request into multiple Fulfillment Requests
- Ensures appropriate fulfillment-related Subscription information is kept up-to-date, such as approval/rejections, modifications, cancellations, and so on
- Enables the recording of patterns of service consumption that can be used to shape demand for new and/or improved services
- Tracks fulfillment status and receives completion notifications from fulfillment channel(s); consumers are able to receive status updates at the Subscription level, not at the level of the underlying requests needed to fulfill the Subscription

(Syllabus Reference: Unit 7, Request to Fulfill Value Stream, Learning Outcome 15: You should be able to briefly describe the data object(s) associated with the Request Rationalization functional component.)

The Request data object contains all Offers from the Shopping Cart which have been consumed and need to be fulfilled.

The Subscription data object represents the rights to access a service that has been provided to a consumer.

8.5.6 Fulfillment Execution Functional Component
(Syllabus Reference: Unit 7, Request to Fulfill Value Stream, Learning Outcome 16: You should be able to explain the purpose of the Fulfillment Execution functional component.)

The Fulfillment Execution functional component:
- Orchestrates the delivery of the various requests amongst (one or more) fulfillment engines in order to deliver the IT service
- Manages a registry of the available fulfillers (e.g., the systems, engaged systems, or external providers that perform actions)
- Takes the bound Service Catalog Entry, and generates both the relevant Fulfillment Requests and the Desired Service data object
- Updates the IT asset inventory as services are ordered
- Requests standard changes and updates the Configuration Management functional component (if needed) on delivery of components
- Maintains visibility into supplier capacity levels and raises alerts if capacity appears to be insufficient for immediate demand

The Fulfillment Execution functional component can be used via two paradigms:
- **Consumer-driven**: A consumer request results in a bound Service Catalog Entry which is broken down into the necessary Fulfillment Requests needed to fulfill the originating request
- **Direct access** (without a Service Catalog Entry): In cases in which there aren't sufficient catalog entries to describe the fulfillment and no entries are planned to be created, the Release Composition functional component (R2D Value Stream) engages and provides enough information to the Fulfillment Execution functional component in order

to create the Fulfillment Request(s) necessary to perform the actions needed

(Syllabus Reference: Unit 7, Request to Fulfill Value Stream, Learning Outcome 17: You should be able to briefly describe the data object(s) associated with the Fulfillment Execution functional component.)

The Fulfillment Request data object describes all fulfillment aspects of an IT service.

The Desired Service data object is the specification of an instance of a service as required to meet the fulfillment requirements detailed in the consumer order (Request) and supported by a single Service Release Blueprint. It contains the relevant parameters that determine how a service will be deployed/fulfilled.

8.5.7 Usage Functional Component

(Syllabus Reference: Unit 7, Request to Fulfill Value Stream, Learning Outcome 18: You should be able to explain the purpose of the Usage functional component.)

The Usage functional component tracks and manages actual usage of subscribed IT services and their associated costs.

(Syllabus Reference: Unit 7, Request to Fulfill Value Stream, Learning Outcome 19: You should be able to briefly describe the data object(s) associated with the Usage functional component.)

The Usage Record data object is the measured use of a particular service or service component.

8.5.8 Chargeback/Showback Functional Component

(Syllabus Reference: Unit 7, Request to Fulfill Value Stream, Learning Outcome 20: You should be able to explain the purpose of the Chargeback/Showback functional component.)

The Chargeback/Showback functional component provides Chargeback or Showback for services based on Subscription, Service Contract, and/or Usage information.

(Syllabus Reference: Unit 7, Request to Fulfill Value Stream, Learning Outcome 21: You should be able to briefly describe the data object(s) associated with the Chargeback/Showback functional component.)

The Chargeback Contract data object details the contract for financial obligations between the service consumer and provider(s) as defined at the time of the subscription.

The Chargeback Record data object represents the actual charge to the subscriber based on the Usage of subscribed services in a given time period.

8.5.9 Knowledge & Collaboration Supporting Function

(Syllabus Reference: Unit 7, Request to Fulfill Value Stream, Learning Outcome 22: You should be able to explain the purpose of the Knowledge & Collaboration supporting function.)

The Knowledge & Collaboration supporting function:
- Provides Knowledge and Conversations that help to address the needs of IT service consumers; this includes articles, conversations from users, webinars, videos, training materials, etc.
- Encourages users and IT staff to contribute to Knowledge in order to reduce the number of requests for information/knowledge that arrive at the IT service desk

(Syllabus Reference: Unit 7, Request to Fulfill Value Stream, Learning Outcome 23: You should be able to briefly describe the data object(s) associated with the Knowledge & Collaboration supporting function.)

The Knowledge data object is structured and unstructured Knowledge from the Knowledge & Collaboration supporting function.

The Conversation data object gathers user Conversations from the Knowledge & Collaboration supporting function.

8.6 Summary

The purpose of the Request to Fulfill Value Stream is to manage catalogs, Subscriptions, and fulfillment across multiple providers.

- It helps an IT organization transition to a service broker model
- It presents a single catalog with items from multiplier supplier catalogs
- It efficiently manages Subscriptions and total cost of service
- It manages and measures fulfillments across multiple suppliers

8.7 Recommended Reading

The following are recommended sources of further information for this chapter:
- The IT4IT Reference Architecture, Version 2.1, Chapter 7

8.8 Exercise 7: Request to Fulfill Value Stream

1. What are the objectives of the R2F Value Stream?

2. What are the benefits of implementing the R2F Value Stream?

3. What are three KPIs for the R2F Value Stream?

4. Complete the first column in the following table, by entering the relevant number(s) to identify the description matching the functional component.

Answer	Functional Component	Description
_____	Offer Consumption	1. Rationalizes the order/request into individual Fulfillment Requests and authorizes Subscriptions.
_____	Catalog Composition	2. Aggregates all Catalog Composition items and external supplier catalogs into consumable Offers that users can order through the Offer Consumption functional component.

Answer	Functional Component	Description
	Fulfillment Execution	3. Represents the modern IT engagement/consumption experience, which exposes a variety of opportunities to acquire services, goods, knowledge, and/or support.
	Chargeback/Showback	4. Routes the individual Fulfillment Requests to the appropriate fulfillment engines.
	Usage	5. Creates, updates, and publishes Service Catalog Entries including all their dependencies necessary to be presented as an Offer in the Offer Management functional component.
	Request Rationalization	6. Presents consumable Offers derived from Service Catalog Entries with associated descriptions, pictures, prices, and purchasing options to prospective consumers.
	Offer Management	7. Provides Chargeback or Showback for services taking into account service Subscription, Service Contract, and/or Usage information.
	Engagement Experience Portal	8. Tracks and manages actual usage of subscribed IT services and their costs.

5. Complete the first column in the following table, by entering the relevant number(s) to identify the data object associated with the functional component.

Answer	Data Object	Functional Component
	Desired Service	1. Chargeback/Showback
	Service Catalog Entry	2. Engagement Experience Portal
	Subscription	3. Usage
	Shopping Cart	4. Catalog Composition
	Usage Record	5. Fulfillment Execution
	Chargeback Contract	6. Request Rationalization
	User Profile	7. Offer Consumption
	Offer	8. Offer Management

8.9 Test Yourself Questions

Q1: Which of the following is an objective of the Request to Fulfill Value Stream?
- A. Creating a blueprint for a streamlined consumption experience that engages consumers
- B. Driving predictable outcomes without driving out innovation
- C. Integrating data within multiple areas of the IT portfolio
- D. Optimizing services provided by bringing together multiple functional areas

Q2: Which of the following is a benefit of implementing the R2F Value Stream?
- A. Ensuring that services are designed in accordance with standards and policies
- B. Improved financial management by providing visibility across service Subscription, Usage, and Chargeback
- C. Increased efficiency by centralized Event Management
- D. Service lifecycle tracking through conceptual, logical, and physical domains

Q3: Which of the following is a KPI for operational performance in the R2F Value Stream?
- A. Number of cancelled purchase orders
- B. Number of completed service requests
- C. Number of security incidents causing financial loss
- D. The software license percentage in use

Q4: Which of the following describes the purpose of the Offer Consumption functional component?
- A. Aggregates all Catalog Composition items and external supplier catalogs into consumable Offers that users can order
- B. Enables the aggregation of catalogs from multiple suppliers into a single Offer Catalog
- C. Presents consumable Offers derived from Service Catalog Entries to prospective consumers
- D. Provides a modern IT engagement/consumption experience, enabling users to acquire services, goods, knowledge, and/or support

Q5: Which functional component within the R2F Value Stream ensures fulfilment-related Subscription information is kept up-to-date?
A. Chargeback/Showback
B. Fulfillment Execution
C. Offer Management
D. Request Rationalization

Q6: Complete the sentence: The _____ data object associated with the _____ functional component contains all Offers from the Shopping Cart, which have been consumed and need to be fulfilled.
A. Fulfillment Request, Fulfillment
B. Offer, Offer Management
C. Request, Request Rationalization
D. User Profile, Offer Management

Q7: What data object only exists during the actual shopping session?
A. Conceptual Service
B. Fulfillment Request
C. Service Design
D. Shopping Cart

Q8: What data object associated with the Offer Management functional component defines how a Service Catalog Entry will be instantiated?
A. Fulfillment Request
B. Offer
C. Service Backlog Item
D. Service Release

Chapter 9

The Detect to Correct Value Stream

9.1 Key Learning Points

This chapter will help you understand the Detect to Correct Value Stream.

Key Points Explained
This chapter will help you to understand and explain:
- The objectives of the value stream
- The benefits of implementing the value stream
- The Key Performance Indicators (KPIs)
- The purpose of the functional components
- The key data objects associated with the functional components

9.2 Objectives

(Syllabus Reference: Unit 8, Detect to Correct Value Stream, Learning Outcome 1: You should be able to describe the objectives of the Detect to Correct (D2C) Value Stream.)

The objectives for the D2C Value Stream are as follows:
- To provide a framework for integrating the work of IT operations in order to enhance IT services and efficiencies
- To provide a comprehensive overview of the business of IT operations and the services delivered by IT operations
- To improve the ability of IT to support business objectives by providing agility, increase uptime, and lower per-service cost

9.3 Benefits

(Syllabus Reference: Unit 8, Request to Fulfill Value Stream, Learning Outcome 2: You should be able to explain the benefits of implementing the D2C Value Stream for the business.)

The benefits of implementing the D2C Value Stream are increased efficiency, reduced cost, reduced risk, and continuous service improvement.

Increased efficiency and reduced cost can be achieved through:
- Focusing response based on causal factor, priority, and business impact
- Increasing sharing of information and reduction of multiple entry of the same data
- Creating a prescriptive data flow between Event, Incident, Problem, and Change Control
- Centralized Event Management for faster analysis
- Automation between and across business functions
- Knowledge management and self-service linkage
- Driving Service Monitoring configuration, operating/service level targets, and predefined Knowledge linked to the R2F Value Stream
- Improving the speed at which issues with a business service are identified; including proactive identification before service impact is severe

Reduced risk can be achieved through:
- Consistent data and configuration information shared between operational silos
- Prescriptive flow semantics and data objects
- Defined business impact
- Reducing the need for best-guess routing and clannish knowledge
- Increased uptime by reduced Mean Time To Repair (MTTR)
- Creating a consistent way of managing Service-Level Management (SLM) definitions, measurements, KPI calculations, and reporting back to the proper service owner or user (in the R2F Value Stream)
- Implementing network security to minimize intrusions that cause denial of service, viruses, and theft or corruption of data and minimize risk exposure
- Utilizing Security Information and Event Management (SIEM) to identify complex attack signatures that can disrupt operations and affect compliance
- Performing threat and vulnerability assessments
- Audit trail
- Clear ownership

Continuous service improvement can be achieved through:
- Defined data objects to be shared with Problem Management
- Using this accumulated Knowledge as input into the S2P Value Stream
- Improved management information and decision-making

9.4 Key Performance Indicators

(Syllabus Reference: Unit 8, Detect to Correct Value Stream, Learning Outcome 3: You should be able to list the KPIs.)

- Achieve operational excellence:
  - Events: Percentage of monitored Configuration Items *versus* unmonitored Configuration Items in the Actual Service, number of Events that cause business disruption, number of escalated Events, number of false positives
  - Incidents: Number of Incidents, number of escalated Incidents, number of false positives
  - Problems: Number of Problems identified, number of Problems eradicated
  - Changes: Number of Change-related outages, number of emergency Changes, number of unplanned Changes
  - Knowledge: Number of Known Errors per version, average number of times each Known Error was read/used
- Improve customer satisfaction:
  - Number of failed Operational-Level Agreements/Service-Level Agreements (OLAs/SLAs)
  - Percentage of availability of critical business systems
  - Mean Time To Repair (MTTR)
  - Mean Time Between Failures (MTBF)
  - Mean Time Between System Incidents
  - Number of Incidents created by users on system performance
  - Percentage of first call Incident resolution
  - Percentage of success rate for user self-fix
- Improve staff effectiveness:
  - Percentage of automatically remediated Events, percentage of Events correlated to a business service
  - Percentage of re-opened Incidents, average time to close an Incident, percentage of automatically remediated Incidents, percentage of rejected Incidents

- Percentage of automatically remediated Changes
- Alignment with business strategy:
  - Number of hours spent on business-critical services
  - Number of business services defined, percentage of business-critical services, percentage of Configuration Items that are not linked to a business service
  - Percentage of business-critical services with defined service level targets

9.5 Functional Components

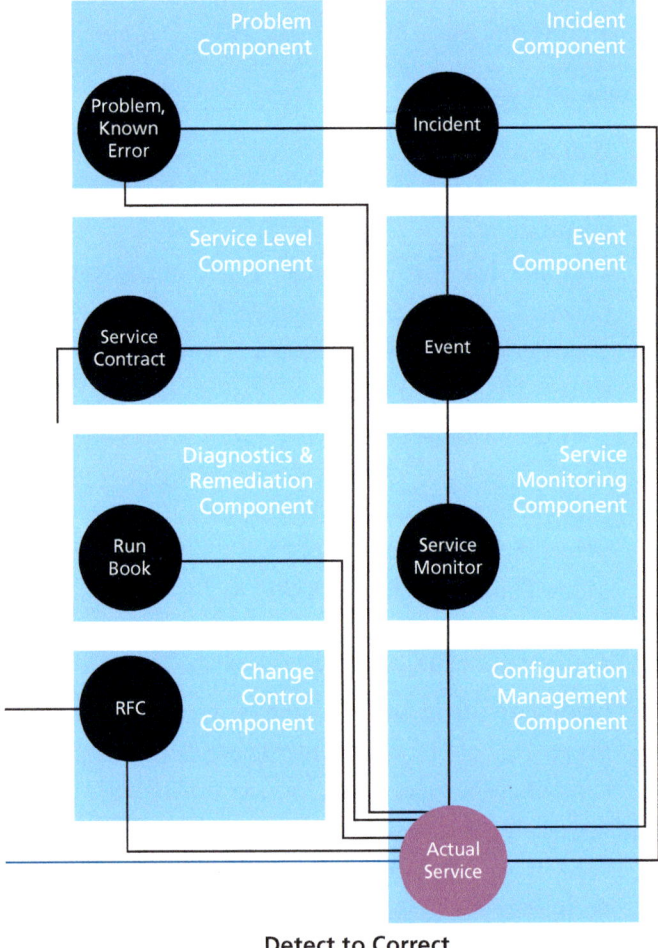

Detect to Correct

Figure 26: D2C Functional Components and Data Objects (Level 1)

The key functional components are:
- Service Monitoring
- Event
- Incident
- Problem
- Change Control
- Configuration Management
- Diagnostics & Remediation
- Service Level

See Appendix D for a summary of the functional components and the data objects in the Detect to Correct Value Stream.

9.5.1 Service Monitoring Functional Component

(Syllabus Reference: Unit 8, Detect to Correct Value Stream, Learning Outcome 5: You should be able to explain the purpose of the Service Monitoring functional component.)

The Service Monitoring function component is in charge of creating, running, and managing monitors that measure all aspects/layers of a service such as infrastructure (system and network), application, and security. It is also in charge of storing all measurement results and calculating compound measurements.

The Service Monitoring functional component is not in charge of the monitor definitions. These are done earlier in the service lifecycle in the R2D Value Stream and are delivered to Service Monitoring by the Fulfillment Execution functional component in the R2F Value Stream.

(Syllabus Reference: Unit 8, Detect to Correct Value Stream, Learning Outcome 6: You should be able to briefly describe the data object(s) associated with the Service Monitoring functional component.)

The Service Monitor data object performs the operational measurement aspects of a Configuration Item or an IT service.

9.5.2 Event Functional Component

(Syllabus Reference: Unit 8, Detect to Correct Value Stream, Learning Outcome 7: You should be able to explain the purpose of the Event functional component.)

The Event functional component manages Events through the Event lifecycle for Events that occur on any IT service. The Event lifecycle includes but is not limited to detecting, categorizing, filtering, analyzing, correlating, logging, prioritizing, and closing Events. During the Event lifecycle some categories of Events can serve as initiators of Incidents and for diagnostics and remediation activities.

(Syllabus Reference: Unit 8, Detect to Correct Value Stream, Learning Outcome 8: You should be able to briefly describe the data object(s) associated with the Event functional component.)

The Event data object represents an alert/notification signifying a change of state of a monitored Configuration Item.

9.5.3 Incident Functional Component

(Syllabus Reference: Unit 8, Detect to Correct Value Stream, Learning Outcome 9: You should be able to explain the purpose of the Incident functional component.)

The Incident functional component facilitates normal service operations restoration as quickly as possible and minimizes the impact on business operations, thus optimizing service quality and availability.

Service restoration can be facilitated through the following means:
- In partnership with the Service Monitoring functional component, filter end-user Interactions and determine which ones should be associated with Incidents
- Incident detection and assessment to investigate the impacts across all domains (e.g., server, network, security, etc.), and determine the correct action to take

- Initiate change and/or remediation activity for some categories of Incidents

An Incident is defined as an unplanned interruption to an IT service or reduction in the quality of an IT service as defined within the Service Contract related to the IT service.

An Interaction is a record of any end-user contact with the service desk agent.

(Syllabus Reference: Unit 8, Detect to Correct Value Stream, Learning Outcome 10: You should be able to briefly describe the data object(s) associated with the Incident functional component.)

The Incident data object hosts and manages Incident data.

The Interaction auxiliary data object hosts the record of an end-user's contact with the service desk.

9.5.4 Problem Functional Component

(Syllabus Reference: Unit 8, Detect to Correct Value Stream, Learning Outcome 11: You should be able to explain the purpose of the Problem functional component.)

The Problem functional component manages the lifecycle of all Problems. The objectives of the Problem functional component are to solve severe/repeating Incidents, prevent Incidents from happening, and minimize the impact of Incidents that cannot be prevented.

The Problem cause is not usually known at the time of the Problem data object instance creation, and the Problem functional component is responsible for the investigation. The Problem functional component also serves as the main exit point from the D2C Value Stream for the feedback information about IT services issues. The feedback is reported to the R2D Value Stream in the form of Defects and to the S2P Value Stream in the form of Portfolio Backlog Items (demand request).

(Syllabus Reference: Unit 8, Detect to Correct Value Stream, Learning Outcome 12: You should be able to briefly describe the data object(s) associated with the Problem functional component.)

The Problem, Known Error data object defines the Problem or Known Error and manages the Problem and Known Error lifecycle.

9.5.5 Change Control Functional Component

(Syllabus Reference: Unit 8, Detect to Correct Value Stream, Learning Outcome 13: You should be able to explain the purpose of the Change Control functional component.)

The Change Control functional component is responsible for managing the lifecycle of all the Requests for Change (RFCs) in the IT environment. It makes sure that changes are done in a standardized way so that the business risk is minimized.

It manages change by facilitating communication with stakeholders and by assessing risk of proposed changes. Furthermore, it enables management of organizational changes and training needed for making a new release a success. Besides, it supports automation of changes so that human participation is minimized and uses a change calendar in order to avoid change conflicts.

(Syllabus Reference: Unit 8, Detect to Correct Value Stream, Learning Outcome 14: You should be able to briefly describe the data object(s) associated with the Change Control functional component)

The RFC data object records data required to manage the change lifecycle. An RFC includes details of the proposed change.

9.5.6 Configuration Management Functional Component

(Syllabus Reference: Unit 8, Detect to Correct Value Stream, Learning Outcome 15: You should be able to explain the purpose of the Configuration Management functional component.)

The Configuration Management functional component tracks the inventories of Actual Services and their associated relationships. It identifies, controls, records, reports, audits, and verifies service items.

(Syllabus Reference: Unit 8, Detect to Correct Value Stream, Learning Outcome 16: You should be able to briefly describe the data object(s) associated with the Configuration Management functional component.)

The Actual Service data object represents the realized deployment of the service, and includes Configuration Items that represent the implemented service components.

9.5.7 Diagnostics & Remediation Functional Component

(Syllabus Reference: Unit 8, Detect to Correct Value Stream, Learning Outcome 17: You should be able to explain the purpose of the Diagnostic & Remediation functional component.)

Through the use of Run Books, the Diagnostics & Remediation functional component provides diagnostics information and/or remediation steps to shorten the Mean Time To Repair (MTTR). Run Books help streamline diagnostics and remediation for service functions by applying knowledge solutions to service anomalies.

(Syllabus Reference: Unit 8, Detect to Correct Value Stream, Learning Outcome 18: You should be able to briefly describe the data object(s) associated with the Diagnostics & Remediation functional component.)

The Run Book data object is a routine compilation of the procedures and operations which the administrator or operator of the system carries out.

9.5.8 Service Level Functional Component

(Syllabus Reference: Unit 8, Detect to Correct Value Stream, Learning Outcome 19: You should be able to explain the purpose of the Service Level functional component.)

The Service Level functional component:
- Enables the design, creation, and management of Service Contracts (SLAs)
- Manages all Service Contract data objects throughout their lifecycle, including the governance of the Service Contract instances from the moment they are instantiated
- Collects the information required to monitor compliance with the terms specified in the Service Contract and exposes data that reflects that actual performance against the defined Service-Level Objectives (SLOs)

The legal aspects of the Service Contracts are not handled by the Service Level functional component directly; however, these documents (usually created and managed by the legal department and not in IT) are used by the functional components in the S2P and R2D Value Streams as the main input for the demand and requirements definition stages.

(Syllabus Reference: Unit 8, Detect to Correct Value Stream, Learning Outcome 20: You should be able to briefly describe the data object(s) associated with the Service Level functional component.)

The Service Contract data object describes the service characteristics and supports service measurement tracking, governance, and audit.

The Key Performance Indicator data object defines an objective that is measured, its requested threshold, and the calculation method to be used.

9.6 Other IT Operations Areas

(Syllabus Reference: Unit 8, Detect to Correct Value Stream, Learning Outcome 21: You should be able to list other IT operations capabilities that are not part of the D2C Value Stream.)

There are other IT operations capabilities that are not part of the D2C Value Stream but have a relationship with it. These include, for example:
- Capacity planning
- Availability management

- Intelligence, trending, proactive alerting (these are within the Service Monitoring functional component)

9.7 Summary

The purpose of the Detect to Correct Value Stream is to integrate IT operations and to quickly find and fix issues within it. The D2C Value Stream:
- Brings together IT service operations to enhance results and efficiency
- Enables end-to-end visibility using a shared configuration model
- Identifies issues before they affect users
- Reduces the MTTR

9.8 Recommended Reading

The following are recommended sources of further information for this chapter:
- The IT4IT Reference Architecture, Version 2.1, Chapter 8

9.9 Exercise 8: Detect to Correct Value Stream

1. What are the objectives of the D2C Value Stream?

2. What are the benefits of implementing the D2C Value Stream?

3. What are three KPIs for the D2C Value Stream?

4. Complete the first column in the following table, by entering the relevant number(s) to identify the description matching the functional component.

Answer	Functional Component	Description
	Change Control	1. Creates, runs, and manages monitors, which measure all aspects/layers of a service such as infrastructure (system and network), application, and security.

Answer	Functional Component	Description
_____	Configuration Management	2. Facilitates normal service operations restoration as quickly as possible and minimizes the impact on business operations, thus optimizing service quality and availability.
_____	Diagnostics & Remediation	3. Manages the lifecycle of all Problems.
_____	Event	4. Enables the design, creation, and management of Service Contracts (SLAs).
_____	Service Level	5. Manages Events through the Event lifecycle for Events that occur on any IT service.
_____	Incident	6. Tracks the inventories of Actual Services and their associated relationships.
_____	Problem	7. Manages the lifecycle of all the RFCs in the IT environment.
_____	Service Monitoring	8. Provides diagnostics information and/ or remediation steps to shorten the MTTR.

5. Complete the first column in the following table, by entering the relevant number(s) to identify the data object associated with the functional component.

Answer	Data Object	Functional Component
_____	Run Book	1. Service Monitoring
_____	RFC	2. Event
_____	Interaction	3. Incident
_____	Actual Service	4. Problem
_____	Key Performance Indicator	5. Change Control
_____	Service Monitor	6. Configuration Management
_____	Event	7. Diagnostics & Remediation
_____	Problem, Known Error	8. Service Level

9.10 Test Yourself Questions

Q1: Which of the following is an objective of the Detect to Correct Value Stream?
   A. Creating a consumption experience that consistently engages consumers
   B. Enabling IT alignment with business plans
   C. Integrating the work of IT operations to enhance services and efficiencies
   D. Standardize service development and delivery so that re-use is the norm

Q2: Which of the following is a benefit of implementing the D2C Value Stream?
   A. Accelerated sourcing and delivery of applications and services
   B. Increased efficiency by centralized Event Management
   C. Reduced complexity in the IT shopping experience
   D. Service lifecycle tracking through conceptual, logical, and physical domains

Q3: Which of the following is a KPI for improving staff effectiveness in the D2C Value Stream?
   A. New Subscriptions per time period
   B. Number of purchase orders per time period
   C. Percentage of re-opened Incidents
   D. The percentage of time invested on business-critical services

Q4: Which of the following describes the purpose of the Incident functional component?
   A. Facilitates normal service operations restoration with minimized impact
   B. Manages the lifecycle of all Problems that occur on any IT service or application
   C. Provides diagnostics information and/or remediation steps
   D. Provides Knowledge to address the needs of IT service consumers

Q5: Which functional component within the D2C Value Stream manages the lifecycle of RFCs?
A. Build
B. Change Control
C. Event
D. Problem

Q6: Complete the sentence: The _____ auxiliary data object associated with the _____ functional component hosts the record of an end-user's contact with the service desk.
A. Event, Diagnostics & Remediation
B. Interaction, Incident
C. RFC, Configuration Management
D. Key Performance Indicator, Service Level

Q7: What data object associated with the Service Monitoring functional component performs operational measurement of an IT service?
A. Actual Service
B. Key Performance Indicator
C. Service Contract
D. Service Monitor

Q8: What data object associated with the D2C Value Stream is a compilation of the procedures and operations which the operator of the system carries out?
A. Artifact
B. Conversation
C. Run Book
D. Remediation Script

Appendix A

Answers to Exercises and Test Yourself Questions

A.1 Answers to Exercises

A.1.1 Exercise 1: IT4IT Overview

In your own words, provide short answers to these questions.

1. What is the IT4IT Reference Architecture and what approach does it use?
   The Open Group IT4IT Reference Architecture is a standard reference architecture for managing the business of IT. It uses a value chain approach to create a model of the functions that IT performs to help organizations identify the activities that contribute to business competitiveness.

2. How should the IT4IT Reference Architecture be used by organizations?
   It should be used as the basis for a standard model for creating an IT management ecosystem, and is intended to help organizations adapt to changes in technology, process, and methods without having to re-factor the management architecture to accommodate every shift.

3. What is the difference between primary activities and supporting activities in the IT Value Chain?
   The primary activities are concerned with the production or delivery of goods or services for which the IT business function is directly accountable. This includes activities such as planning, production, consumption, fulfillment, and support.
   Supporting activities facilitate the efficiency and effectiveness of the primary activities. This includes supporting activities such as finance, human resource, governance, and supplier management. These are activities that are shared across the whole enterprise and are not IT-specific.

4. What are the primary activities of the IT Value Chain?
   The primary activities of the IT Value Chain are known as value streams and are:
   - Strategy to Portfolio
   - Requirement to Deploy
   - Request to Fulfill
   - Detect to Correct

5. What is the difference between a value chain and a value stream?
   A value chain is a series of activities that an organization performs in order to deliver something valuable, such as a product or service. Products pass through activities of the chain in order, and, at each activity, the product gains some value. The value streams can be thought of as the direction functions of the value chain; in the case of the IT Value Chain they can be characterized as Plan, Build, Deliver, and Run.
6. How do the four value streams manage the full service lifecycle?
   Each value stream encapsulates capabilities that are necessary to manage aspects of the service lifecycle. These capabilities are realized as a set of functional components and data objects. The functional components within the four value streams together are responsible for creating, refining, and tracking key data objects across the full service lifecycle.
7. What is the Strategy to Portfolio Value Stream?
   The Strategy to Portfolio (S2P) Value Stream is the "plan" part of the "plan, build, deliver, run" of the IT Value Chain. This activity defines a strategy to balance and broker the IT portfolio: it drives the IT portfolio towards business innovation.
8. What is the Requirement to Deploy Value Stream?
   The Requirement to Deploy (R2D) Value Stream is the "build" part of the "plan, build, deliver, run" of the IT Value Chain. This activity prioritizes every requirement to build the best services and deploy them: it builds what the business needs when it needs it.
9. What is the Request to Fulfill Value Stream?
   The Request to Fulfill (R2F) Value Stream is the "deliver" part of the "plan, build, deliver, run" of the IT Value Chain. This activity handles each request for services through a streamlined process to fulfill it: it catalogs, fulfills, and manages service usage.
10. What is the Detect to Correct Value Stream?
    The Detect to Correct (D2C) Value Stream is the "run" part of the "plan, build, deliver, run" of the IT Value Chain. This activity seeks to detect issues and correct them before impacting users: it anticipates and resolves production issues.

A.1.2 Exercise 2: Definitions

1. Complete the first column in the following table, by entering the relevant number(s) to identify the definition matching the term.

Mapping	Term	Definition
4	Key Data Object	1. Those that are important but not essential to the service lifecycle.
3	System of Insight	2. Primarily used to depict the connections between data objects.
1	Auxiliary Data Object	3. Used to describe relationships between data objects for the purpose of generating knowledge, information, or analytics.
5	Functional Component	4. Those essential to managing or advancing the service lifecycle.
2	Relationship	5. The smallest unit of technology in the IT4IT Reference Architecture that can stand on its own, and be useful as a whole to an IT service provider.

A.1.3 Exercise 3: Basic Concepts

In your own words, provide short answers to these questions.

1. What is the scope of the Strategy to Portfolio Value Stream?

   The Strategy to Portfolio (S2P) Value Stream is focused on planning and choosing the right set of investments that IT should be making in any given period to respond to the demands placed upon it. It provides IT organizations with a framework for interconnecting the different functions involved in managing the portfolio of services delivered to the enterprise. Activities such as capturing demand for IT services, prioritizing and forecasting investments, Service Portfolio Management, and Project Management require data consistency and transparency in order to maintain alignment between the business strategy and the IT portfolio.

2. What is the scope of the Requirement to Deploy Value Stream?

   The Requirement to Deploy (R2D) Value Stream is focused on building or sourcing and turning the investment decisions from the S2P Value Stream into services. It provides the framework for creating/sourcing new services or modifying those that already exist. The R2D Value Stream consumes the Conceptual Service produced in the S2P Value Stream and through a series of design, development or sourcing, and testing functions enables the development of the Logical Service.

3. What is the scope of the Request to Fulfill Value Stream?
   The Request to Fulfill (R2F) Value Stream is a framework connecting the various consumers (business users, IT practitioners, or end customers) with goods and services that are used to satisfy productivity and innovation needs. The R2F Value Stream places emphasis on time-to-value, repeatability, and consistency for consumers looking to request and obtain services from IT. The R2F Value Stream helps IT optimize both service consumption and fulfillment experiences for users by delineating functions for an Offer Catalog and Catalog Composition. The R2F Value Stream framework provides a single consumption experience to consumers for seamless subscription to both internal and external services, as well as managing Subscriptions and routing fulfillments to different service providers using the R2F Value Stream framework.
4. What is the scope of the Detect to Correct Value Stream?
   The Detect to Correct (D2C) Value Stream provides a framework for integrating the monitoring, management, remediation, and other operational aspects associated with realized services and/or those under construction. It also provides a comprehensive overview of the business of IT operations and the services these teams deliver.
5. What are the typical activities of each value stream?
   - S2P: Strategy, Service Portfolio, Demand, and Selection.
   - R2D: Plan & Design, Develop, Test, and Deploy.
   - R2F: Design & Publish, Subscribe, Fulfill and Measure.
   - D2C: Detect, Diagnose, Change, and Resolve.
6. What is the IT4IT Service Model?
   The Service Model construct in the architecture captures, connects, and maintains service lifecycle attributes as the service progresses through its lifecycle. The provider/broker model provided by the IT4IT Service Model places its focus on services as the primary IT deliverable and requires a higher degree of flexibility, velocity, and adaptability.
7. What is the Service Model Backbone?
   The structure that binds the different abstraction levels of the Service Model together is called the "Service Model Backbone". The Service Model Backbone provides the data entities, attributes, and necessary relationships between them to ensure end-to-end traceability of a service from concept to instantiation and consumption.

8. What is the IT4IT Information Model?
   The Information Model comprises the set of service lifecycle data objects and their relationships.
9. What is the IT4IT Functional Model?
   The IT4IT Functional Model is the set of functional components and their relationships.
10. What is the difference between primary functional components and secondary functional components?
    A primary functional component is core to a specific value stream. This means that the functional component plays a key role in the activities of a particular value stream. Without this functional component, the integrity of the data objects and thus the Service Model could not be maintained consistently and efficiently.
    Secondary functional components represent some level of dependency or interaction with a value stream and its data objects. While they interact with a value stream, they are not core to it and are either primary to another value stream or supporting function or represent a capability.

A.1.4 Exercise 4: IT4IT Core

1. Insert the number (1..5) in the Answer column to match the IT4IT Reference Architecture Level:

Answer	Abstraction Level Description
5	Solution Architecture
2	Value Stream Documentation
1	End-to-End Overview
4	Vendor-specific Refinement Architecture
3	Vendor-independent Architecture

2. Why was an informal notation chosen for Levels 1 and 2 of the Reference Architecture?
   Levels 1 and 2 use a simplified class model and an informal notation to introduce and explain concepts. An informal notation was selected at these levels so that non-architects would easily understand the architecture.

3. What are the five core concepts introduced at Level 1 of the Reference Architecture?
   - Value streams
   - Functional components
   - Service lifecycle data objects (key data objects)
   - Service Model Backbone data objects (Service Backbone data objects)
   - Relationships
4. What is the objective of the representation of the Level 1 IT4IT Reference architecture?

   The objective of the IT4IT Reference Architecture is to convey, in a prescriptive fashion, the key data objects, relationships, and components that are foundational for all IT organizations.
5. How does the IT4IT Reference Architecture use the value stream concept?

   The IT4IT Reference Architecture uses the value stream concept as a way of grouping the functional components and data objects together to provide context for where value is being created/delivered.
6. What are the four additional concepts introduced at Reference Architecture Level 2?
   - Relationships between data objects are updated with multiplicity/cardinality attributes (e.g., one-to-one, one-to-many, many-to-many)
   - The concept of data flow between functional components is introduced
   - The data flows are refined to depict integrations to build out the system of record fabric
   - The relationships between capability disciplines and functional components are introduced but they are not part of the normative Reference Architecture and are presented as guidance
7. What are the additional concepts introduced at Reference Architecture Level 3?

   This level adds more details for data object definitions, introducing essential attributes for key data objects. It also introduces the concepts of capability discipline, scenarios, and essential services.
8. What is the notation used for the Level 3 Reference Architecture diagrams?

   Level 3 uses a formal notation, expressed in the ArchiMate modeling language and UML.

9. Who owns and controls Levels 4 and 5 of the Reference Architecture?
   Levels 4 and 5 are owned and controlled by suppliers of IT management products and services.
10. What kind of content might be included in Level 4 of the Reference Architecture?
    Abstraction Level 4 is where the architecture becomes more product design and implementation-oriented. Here, for example, providers of IT management products and services can design/specify their service, interface, and exchange models which should be derived from Level 3 content.

A.1.5 Exercise 5: Strategy to Portfolio Value Stream

1. What are the objectives of the S2P Value Stream?
   - To contribute to business strategy and planning enabling IT alignment with business plans
   - To create an IT portfolio framework that allows IT organizations to optimize services provided to business by bringing together multiple functional areas
   - To provide holistic views of IT portfolio activities through data integrations within multiple areas of the IT portfolio
2. What are the benefits of implementing the S2P Value Stream?
   - Holistic IT portfolio view across the IT PMO and the Enterprise Architecture and Service Portfolio functional components
   - IT portfolio decisions based on business priorities
   - Accurate visibility of business and IT demand
   - IT portfolio data consistency
   - Service lifecycle tracking through conceptual, logical, and physical domains
   - Prioritized IT investment based on all IT portfolio facets including cost/value analysis, impacts on architecture, service roadmap, business priorities, etc.
   - Re-balance IT investments between strategic and operational demand
   - Solid communication with business stakeholders through roadmaps
3. What are three KPIs for the S2P Value Stream?
   - Business and IT alignment; e.g., ratio of new *versus* maintenance service
   - Accurate visibility into demands from the business; e.g., demand requests, types and delivery per service percentage of overall IT budget

- Stewardship of IT investment; e.g., CapEx *versus* OpEx, software license percentage in use
4. Complete the first column in the following table, by entering the relevant number(s) to identify the description matching the functional component.

Answer	Functional Component	Description
5	Enterprise Architecture	1. Logs, maintains, and evaluates all demands (new service, enhancements, defects) coming into IT through a single funnel. Correlates incoming demand to similar existing demand or creates new demand.
1	Portfolio Demand	2. Manages the portfolio of IT proposals that are proposed, approved, active, deferred, or rejected.
4	Service Portfolio	3. Manages the creation, review, approval, and audit of all IT policies.
2	Proposal	4. Manages the entire portfolio of services in plan, transition, production, and retirement.
3	Policy	5. Creates and manages long-term IT investment and execution plan-of-action that are critical to business strategic objectives.

5. Complete the first column in the following table, by entering the relevant number(s) to identify the functional component matching the data object.

Answer	Data Object	Functional Component
3	Portfolio Backlog Item	1. Policy
5	Conceptual Service	2. Proposal
4	Enterprise Architecture	3. Portfolio Demand
2	Scope Agreement	4. Enterprise Architecture
1	Policy	5. Service Portfolio

A.1.6 Exercise 6: Requirement to Deploy Value Stream

1. What are the objectives of the R2D Value Stream?
   - To make service delivery predictable across geographically dispersed teams, multiple suppliers, and multiple development methodologies
   - To ensure that each Service Release is high quality, fit-for-purpose, and meets customer expectations
   - To understand the evolving relationship between planning and building
   - To standardize service development and delivery to the point where re-use of service components is the norm
   - To build a culture of collaboration between IT operations and IT development to support Service Release success
   - To put rigorous information management controls in place to lessen the impact of the IT reality – high staff turnover
   - To drive predictable outcomes without driving out innovation
2. What are the benefits of implementing the R2D Value Stream?
   - Maximize the pipeline of projects and smaller-grained demand requests for faster time-to-market in service realization
   - Predictable outcomes that ensure that the application or service delivered performs as requested, leading to higher rates of user acceptance and better business alignment
   - Establish control points to manage the quality, utility, security, and cost of services, independent of development method or delivery source
   - Increased management information for traceability and benchmarking of internal and external service developers and suppliers
   - Ensure that all services are designed in accordance with standards and policies
   - Improved inputs to IT Financial Management on service cost
   - Relate applications and services with business value by creating and maintaining the service blueprint
   - Accelerate the sourcing and delivery of applications and services through best practices such as re-use, automation, and collaboration
3. What are three KPIs for the R2D Value Stream?
   - Increase automation adoption; e.g., % of automated tests

- Achieve development process excellence; e.g., % of requirements test, % of changes resulting in Incidents, ratio of detected to closed Defects at release
- Improve quality; e.g., % of actual *versus* planned executed tests, % of critical Defects found early in unit testing

4. Complete the first column in the following table, by entering the relevant number(s) to identify the description matching the functional component.

Answer	Functional Component	Description
8	Build	1. Plan, store, and execute tests that ensure that the IT service will support the customer's requirements.
5	Build Package	2. Manages the Release Package, Service Release, Service Release Blueprints, and overall Service Release for developing and delivering new or changed services.
9	Defect	3. Ensures that the source is developed in accordance with design specifications, policies, standards, and non-functional requirements.
6	Project	4. Produces a Logical Service, which describes the service structure and behavior considering both the service system and the service offer.
2	Release Composition	5. Creates a deployable package made up of one or many Builds.
7	Requirement	6. Provides ongoing execution oversight of IT Initiatives aimed at the creation of new or enhancements to existing services.
4	Service Design	7. Manages Requirements through the lifecycle of a service.
3	Source Control	8. Manages the creation, implementation, automation, security and storage of all Builds.
1	Test	9. Manages Defects, keeping track of their status, and their relationships back to Requirements and Known Errors.

5. Complete the first column in the following table, by entering the relevant number(s) to identify the data object associated with the functional component.

Answer	Data Object	Functional Component
6	Logical Service	1. Requirement
8	Build	2. Source Control
5	Service Release Blueprint	3. Project
1	Requirement	4. Build Package
9	Defect	5. Release Composition
7	Test Case	6. Service Design
4	Build Package	7. Test
2	Source	8. Build
3	IT Initiative	9. Defect

A.1.7 Exercise 7: Requirement to Fulfill Value Stream

1. What are the objectives of the R2F Value Stream?
   - To provide a blueprint for creating a streamlined consumption experience that engages consumers and eliminates the need for them to avoid working with their IT organization
2. What are the benefits of implementing the R2F Value Stream?
   - It provides a blueprint for increasing business innovation velocity by facilitating a service consumption experience that allows consumers to easily find and subscribe to goods and services through a self-service engagement model
   - It provides a functional framework that delineates between a single Offer Catalog and multiple Catalog Compositions to reduce complexity in the IT shopping experience
   - It provides an architectural foundation for moving from traditional IT request management to service brokerage that increases both business and IT effectiveness
   - It increases fulfillment efficiency and consistency through standard change deployment and automation

- It provides holistic visibility and traceability across service Subscription, Usage, and Chargeback to improve IT Financial Management
- It enables increased cost optimization; for example, by canceling expired Subscriptions and reclaiming resources, Subscriptions, and/or licenses that are unused

3. What are three KPIs for the R2F Value Stream?
   - Ability to meet customer expectations; e.g., new or modified Subscriptions per time period; % and number of Subscription requests complying or breaching SLA; number of Incidents related to request fulfillment
   - Cost reduction; e.g., costs per service and per fulfillment step; % and number of fulfillments requiring human intervention
   - External service provider compliance; e.g., % and number of orders delivered and accepted complying with contract agreements; number of Incidents related to purchase order fulfillment; number of purchase orders unfulfilled at the end of a given period

4. Complete the first column in the following table, by entering the relevant number(s) to identify the description matching the functional component.

Answer	Functional Component	Description
6	Offer Consumption	1. Rationalizes the order/request into individual Fulfillment Requests and authorizes Subscriptions.
5	Catalog Composition	2. Aggregates all Catalog Composition items and external supplier catalogs into consumable Offers that users can order through the Offer Consumption functional component.
4	Fulfillment Execution	3. Represents the modern IT engagement/consumption experience, which exposes a variety of opportunities to acquire services, goods, knowledge, and/or support.
7	Chargeback/Showback	4. Routes the individual Fulfillment Requests to the appropriate fulfillment engines.

App. A ANSWERS TO EXERCISES AND TEST YOURSELF QUESTIONS

Answer	Functional Component	Description
8	Usage	5. Creates, updates, and publishes Service Catalog Entries including all their dependencies necessary to be presented as an Offer in the Offer Management functional component.
1	Request Rationalization	6. Presents consumable Offers derived from Service Catalog Entries with associated descriptions, pictures, prices, and purchasing options to prospective consumers.
2	Offer Management	7. Provides Chargeback or Showback for services taking into account service Subscription, Service Contract, and/or Usage information.
3	Engagement Experience Portal	8. Tracks and manages actual usage of subscribed IT services and their costs.

5. Complete the first column in the following table, by entering the relevant number(s) to identify the data object associated with the functional component.

Answer	Data Object	Functional Component
5	Desired Service	1. Chargeback/Showback
4	Service Catalog Entry	2. Engagement Experience Portal
6	Subscription	3. Usage
7	Shopping Cart	4. Catalog Composition
3	Usage Record	5. Fulfillment Execution
1	Chargeback Contract	6. Request Rationalization
2	User Profile	7. Offer Consumption
8	Offer	8. Offer Management

A.1.8 Exercise 8: Detect to Correct Value Stream

1. What are the objectives of the D2C Value Stream?
   - To provide a framework to integrating the work of IT operations so as to enhance IT services and efficiencies

- To provide a comprehensive overview of the business of IT operations and the services delivered by IT operations
- To improve the ability of IT to support business objectives by providing agility, increase uptime, and lower per-service cost

2. What are the benefits of implementing the D2C Value Stream?
   - Increased efficiency and reduced cost
   - Reduced risk
   - Continuous service improvement

3. What are three KPIs for the D2C Value Stream?
   - Achieve operational excellence; e.g., number of Incidents, number of escalated Incidents, number of false positives
   - Improve staff effectiveness; e.g., percentage of automatically remediated Events, percentage of Events correlated to a business service
   - Alignment with business strategy; e.g., number of hours spent on business-critical services, number of business services defined, percentage of business-critical services, percentage of Configuration Items that are not linked to a business service

4. Complete the first column in the following table, by entering the relevant number(s) to identify the description matching the functional component.

Answer	Functional Component	Description
7	Change Control	1. Creates, runs, and manages monitors, which measure all aspects/layers of a service such as infrastructure (system and network), application, and security.
6	Configuration Management	2. Facilitates normal service operations restoration as quickly as possible and minimizes the impact on business operations, thus optimizing service quality and availability.
8	Diagnostics & Remediation	3. Manages the lifecycle of all Problems.
5	Event	4. Enables the design, creation, and management of Service Contracts (SLAs).

Answer	Functional Component	Description
4	Service Level	5. Manages Events through the Event lifecycle for Events that occur on any IT service.
2	Incident	6. Tracks the inventories of Actual Services and their associated relationships.
3	Problem	7. Manages the lifecycle of all the RFCs in the IT environment.
1	Service Monitoring	8. Provides diagnostics information and/or remediation steps to shorten the MTTR.

5. Complete the first column in the following table, by entering the relevant number(s) to identify the data object associated with the functional component.

Answer	Data Object	Functional Component
7	Run Book	1. Service Monitoring
5	RFC	2. Event
3	Interaction	3. Incident
6	Actual Service	4. Problem
8	Key Performance Indicator	5. Change Control
1	Service Monitor	6. Configuration Management
2	Event	7. Diagnostics & Remediation
4	Problem, Known Error	8. Service Level

A.2 Answers to the Test Yourself Questions

This section contains a table of the answers to the Test Yourself Questions organized by chapter of the Study Guide.

Reference	Answer	Notes
Chapter 1	Q1. C	These match the principles stated in the Certification Policy document.
	Q2. D	Knowledge of the IT4IT Certification Program is non-examinable.
	Q3. A	The retake policy requires candidates who fail to wait at least one (1) month before another attempt.
Chapter 2	Q1. D	It is a standard reference architecture for managing the business of IT.
	Q2. B	It should be flexible enough to support frequent changes in business models while sturdy enough to track compliance and cost controls.
	Q3. A	The IT Value Chain is the series of activities that IT performs to add value to a business service or IT service.
	Q4. C	Primary activities are those concerned with the production or delivery of goods or services for which IT is directly accountable. This includes planning, production, consumption, fulfillment, and support.
Chapter 3	Q1. C	Key data objects are those that are essential to managing or advancing the service lifecycle.
	Q2. A	System of engagement is the design principle used to describe the relationship between data objects and humans or functional components via a user experience interface.
	Q3. D	A functional component is a software building block. The smallest unit of technology in the IT4IT Reference Architecture that can stand on its own and be useful as a whole to an IT practitioner (or IT service provider).
	Q4. C	The Service Model Backbone consists of key data objects that annotate an aspect of the service model in its conceptual, logical, or physical state.
Chapter 4	Q1. D	The Strategy to Portfolio Value Stream is focused on providing IT organizations with the optimal framework for interconnecting the different functions involved in managing the portfolio of services delivered to the enterprise.

Reference	Answer	Notes
	Q2. B	The Request to Deploy Value Stream has the four typical activities: plan & design, develop, test, and deploy.
	Q3. C	A key value proposition of the R2F Value Stream is to facilitate a holistic view across service Subscription, Usage, and Chargeback.
	Q4. C	The Requirement to Deploy (R2D) Value Stream receives the Conceptual Service and through a series of design, development or sourcing, and testing functions enables the development of the Logical Service.
	Q5. A	The purpose of the D2C Value Stream is to bring IT service operations functions together to enhance IT results and efficiencies.
	Q6. D	The Service Model construct in the architecture captures, connects, and maintains service lifecycle attributes as the service progresses through its lifecycle.
	Q7. C	Service lifecycle data objects are inputs or outputs associated with an IT4IT functional component or a service lifecycle phase; they are uniquely identified, and have a lifecycle of their own; they maintain structured information that allows for relationship tracking and automation.
	Q8. A	Auxiliary data objects are depicted using gray colored circles. The IT4IT Reference Architecture describes eight auxiliary data objects and, while they are important to the IT function, they do not play a vital role in managing the service lifecycle.
Chapter 5	Q1. D	The upper levels (1-3) are vendor-agnostic and provide generic views that are suitable for strategy and planning purposes as well as for creating IT management product roadmaps.
	Q2. B	Levels 1 and 2 use a simplified class model and an informal notation to introduce and explain concepts. An informal notation was selected at these levels so that non-architects would easily understand the architecture.
	Q3. B	In a Level 2 Reference Architecture diagram, the gray-green rectangles rectangles are functional components either from another value stream or they are supporting components.
	Q4. B	A functional component must have defined input(s) and output(s) that are data objects and must have an impact on a key data object; for example, create, update, delete. Typically, a functional component controls and/or manages a single type of data object but this is not dictated by the architecture.

Reference	Answer	Notes
	Q5. A	In UML, the OMG defines artifact as: *"... the specification of a physical piece of information that is used or produced by a software development process, or by deployment and operation of a system."*
	Q6. C	The horizontal line linking the Service Model data objects (purple circles) shows the stages of the service definition, and is known as the Service Model Backbone – it is what provides traceability. It shows how you can trace from a Conceptual Service, to a Logical Service, through to a Desired Service, and then to an Actual Service in production.
	Q7. A	At Reference Architecture abstraction Level 2 the concept of data flow between functional components is introduced.
	Q8. A	At abstraction Level 3 a formal notation using the ArchiMate language and UML is the primary method for communicating the IT4IT Reference Architecture specification.
Chapter 6	Q1. B	One of the objectives of the S2P Value Stream is to contribute to business strategy and planning enabling IT alignment with business plans.
	Q2. A	A benefit for adopting the S2P Value Stream is accurate visibility of business and IT demand.
	Q3. C	A KPI for business and IT alignment in the S2P Value Stream is the ratio of new *versus* maintenance services.
	Q4. B	The Portfolio Demand functional component logs, maintains, and evaluates all demands (new service, enhancements, defects) coming into IT through a single funnel. It correlates incoming demand to similar existing demand or creates new demand.
	Q5. D	The Proposal functional component manages the portfolio of IT proposals that are proposed, approved, active, deferred, or rejected.
	Q6. D	The Scope Agreement data object associated with the Proposal functional component reflects budget, cost/benefit projections, scope, and other key attributes of proposed work created from rationalized Portfolio Backlog Items.
	Q7. B	The Enterprise Architecture data object includes references to collateral in the target state architecture landscape representing planned and deployed IT services.
	Q8. A	The Conceptual Service represents the business perspective of the service and is the service interaction or the business capability of the service.

Reference	Answer	Notes
Chapter 7	Q1. C	One objective of the R2D Value Stream is to ensure that each Service Release is high quality, fit-for-purpose, and meets customer expectations.
	Q2. B	A benefit of the R2D Value Stream is that it ensures that all services are designed in accordance with standards and policies (from sources including Corporate Compliance, Enterprise Architecture, Risk Management, IT Financial Management, and so on).
	Q3. D	A KPI in the R2D Value Stream for improving stewardship of IT investment is percentage of actual *versus* planned project cost.
	Q4. D	The Service Design functional component produces a Logical Service, which describes the service structure and behavior considering both the service system and the service offer.
	Q5. C	The Project functional component provides ongoing execution oversight of IT Initiatives aimed at the creation of new or enhancements to existing services.
	Q6. D	The Service Release data object associated with the Release Composition functional component represents a planned release of a version of the service system.
	Q7. C	The Source data object is the created or purchased solution to meet the requirements for a particular Service Release.
	Q8. B	The IT Initiative data object details the scope of work to be performed and created from and associated with the Scope Agreement.
Chapter 8	Q1. A	One objective of the R2F Value Stream is to provide a blueprint for creating a streamlined consumption experience that consistently engages consumers and eliminates the need for them to avoid working with their IT organization.
	Q2. B	A benefit of the R2F Value Stream is that it provides holistic visibility and traceability across service Subscription, Usage, and Chargeback to improve IT Financial Management.
	Q3. B	A KPI for operational performance in the R2F Value Stream is the number of completed service requests.
	Q4. C	The Offer Consumption functional component presents consumable Offers derived from Service Catalog Entries with associated descriptions, pictures, prices, and purchasing options to prospective consumers.

Reference	Answer	Notes
	Q5. D	The Request Rationalization function component ensures appropriate fulfillment-related Subscription information is kept up-to-date, such as approval/rejections, modifications, cancellations, and so on.
	Q6. C	The Request data object associated with the Request Rationalization functional component contains all Offers from the Shopping Cart, which have been consumed and need to be fulfilled.
	Q7. D	The Shopping Cart data object contains the IT services that the user wants to order; this object only exists during the actual shopping session.
	Q8. B	The Offer data object associated with the Offer Management functional component defines how a Service Catalog Entry will be instantiated and under what terms and conditions – price, deployment, approval, workflow, service level (contract), etc.
Chapter 9	Q1. C	An objective of the D2C Value Stream is to provide a framework for integrating the work of IT operations so as to enhance IT services and efficiencies.
	Q2. B	A benefit of the D2C Value Stream is increased efficiency and cost reduction through centralized Event Management for faster analysis.
	Q3. C	A KPI for staff effectiveness in the D2C Value Stream is the percentage of re-opened Incidents.
	Q4. A	The Incident function component facilitates normal service operations restoration as quickly as possible and minimizes the impact on business operations, thus optimizing service quality and availability.
	Q5. B	The Change Control functional component manages the lifecycle of all the RFCs in the IT environment.
	Q6. B	The Interaction auxiliary data object associated with the Incident functional component hosts the record of an end-user's contact with the service desk.
	Q7. D	The Service Monitor data object performs the operational measurement aspects of a CI or an IT service.
	Q8. C	The Run Book data object is a routine compilation of the procedures and operations which the administrator or operator of the system carries out.

Appendix B
Test Yourself Examination Paper

B.1 Examination Paper

The purpose of this appendix is to provide an examination paper that will allow you to assess your readiness to take the IT4IT Part 1 Examination.

Preparation for this Examination Paper

Prior to attempting this examination paper you should have worked through this Study Guide section by section, answering the Test Yourself Questions and reading the referenced sections from the IT4IT Reference Architecture. If you have completed your preparation, then you can attempt this examination paper. If not, please spend some time preparing as suggested.

B.2 Questions

The examination paper provided in this appendix uses a simple multiple-choice format, which is the same as the certification examination. Each question has one single correct answer that scores one point.

Please read each question carefully before reading the answer options. Be aware that some questions may seem to have more than one right answer, but you are to look for the one that makes the most sense and is the most correct.

See Appendix C for the answers.

Item 1
Which of the following describes the IT4IT Reference Architecture?
A. A set of best practices for IT Service Management
B. A supporting toolset for managing the business of IT
C. A value chain approach to model the functions that IT performs
D. A vendor-specific model for deploying and running IT services

Item 2

Which statement describes the Strategy to Portfolio (S2P) Value Stream?

A. It provides a framework for integrating the monitoring, managing, and other operational aspects associated with realized services.
B. It receives demands for new or improved services from the business and develops the Conceptual Service.
C. It designs and develops the Logical Service with more detailed requirements to describe the service requested.
D. It is responsible for the tasks to transition a service into production.

Item 3

What are data objects?

A. They are used to capture context for where value is being created and delivered by functional components.
B. They are equivalent to relations as defined in relational algebra.
C. They are tangible items that are owned, consumed, produced, or modified by functional components.
D. They are defined in object-oriented languages such as Java, and are supported by functional components.

Item 4

What are abstraction Levels 3 and 4 of the IT4IT Reference Architecture, respectively?

A. End-to-End Overview, Vendor-specific Foundation Architecture
B. Solution Architecture, Vendor-specific Reference Architecture
C. Value-Stream Documentation, Vendor-specific Documentation
D. Vendor-independent Architecture, Vendor-specific Refinement Architecture

Item 5

What is a benefit of implementing the S2P Value Stream?

A. Balanced IT investment between strategic and operational demand
B. Improved speed at which issues with a business service are detected
C. Reduced complexity in the IT shopping experience
D. Services designed in accordance with standards and policies

Item 6
What are KPIs of the R2D Value Stream?
A. Increase percentage of time spent on business-critical systems; increased uptime of business-critical systems
B. Percentage of automated tests; percentage of budget at risk
C. Percentage of Subscription requests complying with the SLA; arrival and departure rate of service requests
D. Planned *versus* actual service costs; frequency of security assessments

Item 7
What is the purpose of the Offer Management functional component?
A. Aggregating Catalog Composition items and supplier catalogs into consumable Offers
B. Connecting consumers with the right information, goods, and services
C. Enabling the aggregation of catalogs from multiple suppliers into a single Offer Catalog
D. Presenting consumable Offers derived from Service Catalog entries

Item 8
What is a benefit of implementing the D2C Value Stream?
A. Accelerated sourcing and delivery of applications and services through best practices
B. Decision-making based on business priorities
C. Increased fulfillment efficiency and consistency through standard change deployment and automation
D. Reduced risk through consistent configuration information shared between operational silos

Item 9
What concept is introduced at abstraction Level 2 of the Reference Architecture?
A. Capability maps as guidance material
B. Data flow between functional components
C. Scenarios as narratives
D. The Service Model Backbone providing traceability

Item 10
What is a benefit of implementing the R2F Value Stream?
A. Balanced and prioritized IT investment
B. Improved speed at which issues with a business service are detected
C. Reduced complexity in the IT shopping experience
D. Services designed in accordance with standards

Item 11
Complete the sentence: A value chain is a(n) _____.
A. business analysis perspective that describes resources and roles
B. operating model for the business of IT
C. lean-management method for analyzing state for a series of events
D. sequence of activities performed to deliver some value

Item 12
What value stream includes the typical activities: change and resolve?
A. D2C
B. R2D
C. R2F
D. S2P

Item 13
What is an objective of the R2D Value Stream?
A. To enable timely identification and prioritization of an issue.
B. To increase efficiency through standard change deployment and automation.
C. To standardize service delivery to the point where re-use of service components in the norm.
D. To use well-defined system of records to support accurate visibility into business and IT demand.

Item 14
Why was an informal notation chosen for abstraction Levels 1 and 2 of the IT4IT Reference Architecture?
A. To allow all the concepts to be visible on a single slide.
B. To allow non-architects to easily understand the architecture.

C. To introduce and explain concepts using a similar approach to other frameworks.
D. To provide a holistic model of the IT4IT Reference Architecture.

Item 15
What is an objective of the S2P Value Stream?
A. Creating a streamlined consumption experience
B. Providing holistic views of IT portfolio activities
C. Standardizing service development and delivery
D. Understanding the relationship between planning and building

Item 16
What is a benefit of implementing the R2D Value Stream?
A. Improved communication with business stakeholders through roadmaps
B. It provides an architectural foundation to move to a service brokerage model
C. The ability to relate services with business value by creating a service blueprint
D. The ability to re-balance IT investments between strategic and operational demand

Item 17
What data object is an authoritative source for the consolidated set of technical capabilities and specific options available from a service system, which can be delivered by the service provider?
A. Fulfillment Request
B. Offer Catalog
C. Service Catalog Entry
D. Shopping Cart

Item 18
What data object represents a notification signifying a change of state of a monitored Configuration Item?
A. Defect
B. Event
C. Incident
D. Problem/Known Error

Item 19
Complete the sentence: The constituent parts of the system of record fabric for IT management are the _____.
A. data objects and the relationships between them
B. functional components and the value streams
C. incident records, training videos, and project plans
D. IT4IT Functional Model and the associated data flows

Item 20
What is a KPI for the R2F Value Stream?
A. Accounting records are produced to show spend in each service
B. Increased rate of first call resolution
C. New or modified Subscriptions per time period
D. Percentage of actual *versus* planned executed tests

Item 21
Which of the following describes an intended use of the IT4IT Reference Architecture?
A. As a detailed API implementation standard for developers
B. As a security and risk best practice guide for organizations
C. As design guidance for suppliers of products and services
D. As an industry standard for cloud conformance criteria

Item 22
What term describes the set of functional components and their relationships?
A. The IT4IT Functional Model
B. The IT4IT Information Model
C. The IT Value Chain
D. The Service Model Backbone

Item 23
Which of the following describes the IT4IT Service Model?
A. It governs technology deployments.
B. It maintains service lifecycle attributes.
C. It manages delivery and implementation of technology resources.
D. It organizes the IT lifecycle around projects.

Item 24
Complete the sentence: In the Level 1 Class Model, both types of data objects are considered to be _____.
A. functional components
B. Service Backbone data objects
C. service lifecycle data objects
D. value streams

Item 25
Which of the following describes the Conceptual Service data object?
A. A representation of the business perspective of the service
B. An instantiation of the unbound Service Catalog Entry
C. The data store for the realization of the service in the production environment
D. The logical design of the service based on its requirements and the Conceptual Service Blueprint

Item 26
What is the purpose of the Project functional component?
A. Controlling the Chargeback Contract, providing Chargeback or Showback
B. Evaluating all demands coming into IT, such as new service, enhancements, and defects
C. Management of the lifecycle of all RFCs in the IT environment
D. Ongoing oversight of IT Initiatives to create new or enhanced services

Item 27
What does the Desired Service data object represent?
A. The specification of an instance of a service that meets the fulfilment requirements
B. The logical design of the service based on the Conceptual Service
C. Services planned, in transition, in production, or retired
D. The data store for the realization of the service in the production environment

Item 28

Complete the sentence: The Problem functional component may provide feedback in the form of a Portfolio Backlog Item to the _____.

A. D2C Value Stream
B. R2D Value Stream
C. R2F Value Stream
D. S2P Value Stream

Item 29

What do the purple circles and the purple line represent in the Level 1 Reference Architecture Model?

A. Auxiliary data objects and their relationships
B. Lifecycle data objects and relationships
C. Primary functional components and their key data objects
D. Service Model data objects and the Service Backbone

Item 30

What functional component manages the portfolio of IT proposals that are proposed, approved, active, deferred, or rejected?

A. Portfolio Demand
B. Proposal
C. Project
D. Service Portfolio

Item 31

Which of the following is considered to be a primary activity in the IT Value Chain?

A. Administration
B. Compliance
C. Governance
D. Planning

Item 32

Complete the sentence: The Requirement to Deploy Value Stream _____.

A. brings together IT service operations to enhance results and efficiency
B. manages and measures fulfillments across multiple suppliers

C. presents a single catalog with items from multiple suppliers
D. supports agile and traditional development methods

Item 33
Complete the sentence: A key data object _____.
A. describes aspects of how services are created, delivered, and consumed
B. does not play a vital role in managing the service lifecycle
C. identifies and defines an essential building block
D. provides the why, when, and where attributes for a service, and is depicted in purple

Item 34
Complete the sentence: A functional component must have _____.
A. a direct relationship to data entities in the Service Model Backbone
B. alignment with a supporting capability
C. an informal and formal representation
D. defined inputs, outputs, and an impact on a key data object

Item 35
What is the purpose of the Enterprise Architecture functional component?
A. To ensure that the source is developed in accordance with policies, standards, and non-functional requirements.
B. To manage long-term IT investment and the execution plan-of-action.
C. To manage requirements through the lifecycle of a service.
D. To provide ongoing execution oversight of IT Initiatives.

Item 36
What data object is the created or purchased solution to meet the requirements for a particular Service Release?
A. Build Package
B. IT Initiative
C. Source
D. Service Release

Item 37

What is an objective of the D2C Value Stream?

A. Improving the ability of IT to support the business by providing agility and increased uptime.
B. Making service delivery predictable across different suppliers and methodologies.
C. Optimizing services by bringing together multiple functional areas.
D. Providing holistic views of IT portfolio activities through data integrations within multiple areas.

Item 38

What functional component enables the design, creation, and management of Service Contracts?

A. Service Catalog
B. Service Design
C. Service Level
D. Service Portfolio

Item 39

Who owns and controls abstraction Levels 4 and 5 of the Reference Architecture?

A. Formal notation owners including the OMG and The Open Group
B. IT Service Management process owners
C. Suppliers of IT management products and services
D. The Open Group IT4IT Forum

Item 40

What is an objective of the R2D Value Stream?

A. To contribute to IT alignment with business planning.
B. To ensure that each Service Release meets customer expectations.
C. To optimize services provided to business by bringing together multiple functional areas.
D. To support data integrations within multiple areas of the IT Portfolio.

Appendix C

Test Yourself Examination Paper Answers

This appendix contains the answers to the Examination Paper in Appendix B.

C.1 Scoring the Examination

For each question, award yourself one point for each correct answer.

The target score for this examination is 28 points or more out of 40 (70%). Note that at the time of writing the certification examination has a pass mark lower than this examination, so if you can make the target you should be ready to take the real examination.

C.2 Answers

Item 1   C
The IT4IT Reference Architecture uses a value chain approach to model the functions that IT performs, in order to help organizations identify the activities that contribute to business competitiveness.

Item 2   B
The Strategy to Portfolio (S2P) Value Stream receives strategic demands for new or improved services and develops the Conceptual Service.

Item 3   C
Data objects represent tangible, non-trivial data items that are owned, consumed, produced, or modified by the functional components.

Item 4   D
Level 3 describes the comprehensive normative Reference Architecture in the formal ArchiMate language and is known as the Vendor-independent Architecture. Level 4 is vendor-specific and known as the Vendor-specific Refinement Architecture.

Item 5   A

Balanced IT investment based on strategic and operational demands is a benefit of the S2P Value Stream.

Item 6   B

KPIs of the R2D Value Stream include percentage of automated tests (increased automation adoption) and percentage of budget at risk (improved stewardship of IT investment).

Item 7   A

The Offer Management functional component aggregates all Catalog Composition items and external supplier catalogs into consumable Offers that users can order through the Offer Consumption functional component.

Item 8   D

A benefit of implementing the D2C Value Stream is reduced risk through consistent data and configuration information shared between operational silos.

Item 9   B

Abstraction Level 2 introduces the concept of data flow between functional components.

Item 10   C

A benefit of implementing the R2F Value Stream is reduced complexity in the IT shopping experience.

Item 11   D

A value chain is a sequence of activities performed by an organization in order to deliver something valuable, such as a product or service. As the product or service passes through each of the activities, it gains some value.

Item 12   A

The D2C Value Stream includes the four typical activities: Detect, Diagnose, Change, and Resolve.

Item 13   C
An objective of the R2D Value Stream is to standardize service development and delivery to the point where re-use of service components is the norm.

Item 14   B
Levels 1 and 2 use a simplified class model and an informal notation to introduce and explain concepts. An informal notation is used at these levels so that non-architects can easily understand the architecture.

Item 15   B
An objective of the S2P Value Stream is to provide holistic views of IT portfolio activities through data integrations within multiple areas of the IT portfolio.

Item 16   C
A benefit of implementing the R2D Value Stream is that it provides the ability to relate applications and services with business value by creating and maintaining a service blueprint.

Item 17   C
The Service Catalog Entry data object is the authoritative source for the consolidated set of technical capabilities and specific options available from a service system, which can be delivered by the service provider. It serves as the bridge between the service system and the service offer.

Item 18   B
An Event represents an alert/notification signifying a change of state of a monitored CI (D2C Value Stream).

Item 19   A
The data objects, combined with their relationships and inter-dependencies, form the "system of record fabric" for IT management.

Item 20   C
A KPI for the R2F Value Stream is new or modified Subscriptions per time period which is a measure of the ability to meet customer expectations.

Item 21   C

The IT4IT Reference Architecture is intended to function as design guidance for suppliers of IT management products and services.

Item 22   A

The IT4IT Functional Model is the set of functional components and their relationships.

Item 23   B

The Service Model construct captures, connects, and maintains service lifecycle attributes as a service progresses through its lifecycle.

Item 24   C

An important point to understand from the class model is that both types of data objects are considered service lifecycle data objects. This means that the "Service Backbone data objects" that are used to represent the Service Model are a type of lifecycle data object.

Item 25   A

The Conceptual Service represents the business perspective of the service and is the service interaction or the business capability of the service. It is the level suitable for discussing aspects that characterize the service as the product of IT activity including business value, investment history and outlook, value earned, and return on investment. It is abstracted from any technical detail and described in terms that are understood by CxO-level persons who decide on the assignment of budget and resources in order to build and maintain the service.

Item 26   D

The Project functional component coordinates the creation and provides ongoing execution oversight of IT Initiatives aimed at the creation of new or enhancements to existing services.

Item 27   A

The Desired Service data object from the Fulfillment Execution component in the R2F Value Stream is the specification of an instance of a service as required to meet the fulfilment requirements detailed in the consumer order

(Request) and supported by a single Service Release Blueprint. It contains the relevant parameters that determine how a service will be deployed/fulfilled.

Item 28   D
The Problem functional component serves as the main exit point from the D2C Value Stream for the feedback information about IT services issues. The feedback is reported to the R2D Value Stream in the form of Defects and to the S2P Value Stream in the form of Portfolio Backlog Items (demand request).

Item 29   D
The Service Model data objects are shown as purple circles. The horizontal purple line linking these shows the stages of the service definition, and is known as the Service Backbone – it is what provides traceability.

Item 30   B
The Proposal functional component within S2P manages the portfolio of IT proposals that are proposed, approved, active, deferred, or rejected.

Item 31   D
Primary activities are concerned with the production of goods or the delivery of services for which a business function, like IT, is directly accountable. This includes activities such as planning, production, consumption, fulfillment, and support.

Item 32   D
The R2D Value Stream supports agile and traditional development methods.

Item 33   A
Key data objects describe aspects of "how" services are created, delivered, and consumed; they are essential to managing the service lifecycle. Managing the end-to-end service lifecycle and associated measurement, reporting, and traceability would be virtually impossible without them. The IT4IT Reference Architecture defines 32 key data objects and most are depicted as black circles.

Item 34   D

Functional components must have defined input(s) and output(s) that are data objects and must have an impact on a key data object; for example, create, update, or delete. Typically, a functional component controls and/or manages a single type of data object but this is not dictated by the architecture.

Item 35   B

The Enterprise Architecture functional component is in charge of the creation and management of long-term IT investment and execution plan-of-action that are critical to business strategic objectives.

Item 36   C

The Source data object (from the Source Control functional component) is the created or purchased solution to meet the requirements for a particular Service Release.

Item 37   A

An objective of the D2C Value Stream is to improve the ability of IT to support business objectives by providing agility, increase uptime, and lower per-service cost.

Item 38   C

The Service Level functional component in the D2C Value Stream enables the design, creation, and management of Service Contracts (SLAs). It is also responsible for the management of all Service Contract data objects throughout their lifecycle including the governance of the Service Contract instances from the moment they are instantiated.

Item 39   C

Levels 4 and 5 are owned and controlled by suppliers of IT management products and services. The IT4IT Reference Architecture has no direct control over defining and/or approving content at these abstraction levels.

Item 40   B

An objective of the R2D Value Stream is to ensure that each Service Release is fit-for-purpose and meets customer expectations.

Appendix D
Functional Component & Data Object Summary

This appendix contains a summary of the functional components and data objects in the IT4IT Reference Architecture.

D.1 Functional Components

Value Stream	Functional Component	Summary of Purpose	Data Object(s)
S2P	Enterprise Architecture	Creates and manages long-term IT investment and execution plan-of-action that are critical to business strategic objectives.	Enterprise Architecture
	Policy	Manages the creation, review, approval, and audit of all IT policies.	Policy
	Proposal	Manages the portfolio of IT proposals that are proposed, approved, active, deferred, or rejected.	Scope Agreement
	Portfolio Demand	Logs, maintains, and evaluates all demands (new service, enhancements, defects) coming into IT through a single funnel. Correlates incoming demand to similar existing demand or creates new demand.	Portfolio Backlog Item
	Service Portfolio	Manages the entire portfolio of services in plan, transition, production, and retirement.	Conceptual Service
	IT Investment Portfolio (auxiliary functional component)	Manages the portfolio of all authorized IT investments pertaining to a service.	IT Budget Item

Value Stream	Functional Component	Summary of Purpose	Data Object(s)
R2D	Project	Provides ongoing execution oversight of IT Initiatives aimed at the creation of new or enhancements to existing services.	IT Initiative
	Requirement	Manages Requirements through the lifecycle of a service.	Requirement
	Service Design	Produces a Logical Service, which describes the service structure and behavior considering both the service system and the service offer.	Logical Service
	Source Control	Ensures that the source is developed in accordance with design specifications, policies, standards, and non-functional requirements.	Source
	Build	Manages the creation, implementation, automation, security, and storage of all Builds.	Build
	Build Package	Creates a deployable package made up of one or many Builds.	Build Package
	Release Composition	Manages the Release Package, Service Release, Service Release Blueprints, and overall Service Release for developing and delivering new or changed services.	Service Release Service Release Blueprint
	Test	Plan, store, and execute tests that ensure that the IT service will support the customer's requirements.	Test Case
	Defect	Manages Defects, keeping track of their status, and their relationships back to Requirements and Known Errors.	Defect

App. D FUNCTIONAL COMPONENT & DATA OBJECT SUMMARY

Value Stream	Functional Component	Summary of Purpose	Data Object(s)
R2F	Engagement Experience Portal (secondary functional component)	Represents the modern IT engagement/consumption experience, which exposes a variety of opportunities to acquire services, goods, knowledge, and/or support.	User Profile
	Offer Consumption	Presents consumable Offers derived from Service Catalog Entries with associated descriptions, pictures, prices, and purchasing options to prospective consumers.	Shopping Cart
	Offer Management	Aggregates all Catalog Composition items and external supplier catalogs into consumable Offers that users can order through the Offer Consumption functional component.	Offer Offer Catalog (auxiliary)
	Catalog Composition	Enables the aggregation of catalogs from multiple suppliers into a single Offer Catalog and the composition of Service Catalog Entries. Service Catalog Entries are created from the provider point of view and may have some level of fulfillment details exposed.	Service Catalog Entry
	Request Rationalization	Rationalizes the order/request into individual Fulfillment Requests and authorizes Subscriptions.	Request Subscription
	Fulfillment Execution	Routes the individual Fulfillment Requests to the appropriate fulfillment engines.	Fulfillment Request Desired Service
	Usage	Tracks the service Usage.	Usage Record
	Chargeback/ Showback	Controls the Chargeback Contract, providing Chargeback or Showback, for services taking into account service Subscription and Usage information.	Chargeback Contract Chargeback Record
	Knowledge & Collaboration (supporting function)	Provides Knowledge and Conversations that help to address the needs of IT service consumers.	Knowledge Conversation

Value Stream	Functional Component	Summary of Purpose	Data Object(s)
D2C	Service Monitoring	Creates, runs, and manages monitors, which measure all aspects/layers of a service such as infrastructure (system and network), application, and security.	Service Monitor
	Event	Manages Events through the Event lifecycle for Events that occur on any IT service.	Event
	Incident	Facilitates normal service operations restoration as quickly as possible and minimizes the impact on business operations, thus optimizing service quality and availability.	Incident Interaction
	Problem	Manages the lifecycle of all Problems.	Problem, Known Error
	Change Control	Manages the lifecycle of all the RFCs in the IT environment.	RFC
	Configuration Management	Tracks the inventories of Actual Services and their associated relationships.	Actual Service
	Diagnostics & Remediation	Provides diagnostics information and/or remediation steps to shorten the MTTR.	Run Book
	Service Level	Enables the design, creation, and management of Service Contracts (SLAs).	Service Contract Key Performance Indicator

D.2 Data Objects

Value Stream	Data Object	Summary	Functional Component
S2P	Enterprise Architecture	Includes references to collateral in the target state architecture landscape representing planned and deployed IT services.	Enterprise Architecture
	Policy	A central repository for storing and organizing all types of IT policies based on various templates and classification criteria.	Policy
	Scope Agreement	Reflects budget, cost/benefit projections, scope, and other key attributes of proposed work created from approved rationalized Portfolio Backlog Items.	Proposal
	Portfolio Backlog Item	Represents the repository of all incoming demands including but not limited to new requests, enhancement requests, and defect fix requests.	Portfolio Demand
	Conceptual Service	Represents services planned, in transition, in production, or retired.	Service Portfolio
	Conceptual Service Blueprint	Contains the list of all service blueprints associated with a given Conceptual Service.	Service Portfolio
	IT Budget Item	The approved IT investment pertaining to a proposed scope of work.	IT Investment Portfolio
R2D	IT Initiative	Details the scope of the work to be performed and created from and associated with the Scope Agreement.	Project
	Requirement	Details of the needs or conditions to meet for a new or altered service.	Requirement
	Logical Service	Represents the grouping of logical components necessary to provide the expected outcome or service interaction.	Service Design

Value Stream	Data Object	Summary	Functional Component
	Source	The created or purchased solution to meet the requirements for a particular Service Release.	Source Control
	Build	Created from Source and versioned	Build
	Build Package	A compilation of one or many Builds in a deployable package.	Build Package
	Service Release	Represents a planned release of a version of the service system.	Release Composition
	Service Release Blueprint	Provides the planned design/configuration of the components of the service system.	Release Composition
	Test Case	Used to validate that the Service Release is fit-for-purpose	Test
	Defect	An issue with the Service Release Blueprint, which should be remediated to fulfill the associated Requirements.	Defect
R2F	User Profile	Personal data associated with a specific user and the explicit digital representation of a person's identity.	Engagement Experience Portal (secondary functional component)
	Shopping Cart	Contains the IT services that the user wants to order; the object only exists during the actual shopping session.	Offer Consumption
	Offer	Defines how a Service Catalog Entry will be instantiated and under what terms and conditions – price, deployment, approval, workflow, service level (contract), etc.	Offer Management
	Offer Catalog	A set or collection of Offers that are grouped together as something that can be consumed by certain consumers or consumer groups.	Offer Management

App. D FUNCTIONAL COMPONENT & DATA OBJECT SUMMARY

Value Stream	Data Object	Summary	Functional Component
	Service Catalog Entry	An authoritative source for the consolidated set of technical capabilities and specific options available from a service system, which can be delivered by the service provider. It serves as the bridge between the service system and the service offer.	Catalog Composition
	Request	Contains all Offers from the Shopping Cart, which have been consumed and need to be fulfilled.	Request Rationalization
	Subscription	Represents the rights to access a service that has been provided to a consumer.	Request Rationalization
	Fulfillment Request	Describes all fulfillment aspects of an IT service	Fulfillment Execution
	Desired Service	An instantiation of the unbound Service Catalog Entry. This results in a single realized deployment for the service.	Fulfillment Execution
	Usage Record	The measured use of a particular service or service component.	Usage
	Chargeback Contract	Details the financial obligations between the service consumer and provider(s).	Chargeback/ Showback
	Chargeback Record	Represents the actual charge to the subscriber based on the Usage of subscribed services in a given time period.	Chargeback/ Showback
	Knowledge	Structured and unstructured Knowledge from the Knowledge & Collaboration supporting function.	Knowledge & Collaboration (supporting function)
	Conversation	Gathers user conversations from the Knowledge & Collaboration supporting function.	Knowledge & Collaboration (supporting function)

Value Stream	Data Object	Summary	Functional Component
D2C	Service Monitor	Performs the operational measurement aspects of a CI or an IT service.	Service Monitoring
	Event	Represents an alert/notification signifying a change of state of a monitored CI.	Event
	Incident	Hosts and manages Incident data.	Incident
	Interaction	Hosts the record of an end-user's contact with the service desk.	Incident
	Problem, Known Error	Defines the Problem or Known Error and manages the Problem and Known Error lifecycle.	Problem
	RFC	Records data required to manage the change lifecycle. An RFC includes details of the proposed change.	Change Control
	Actual Service	Represents the realized deployment of the service.	Configuration Management
	Run Book	A routine compilation of the procedures and operations which the administrator or operator of the system carries out.	Diagnostics & Remediation
	Service Contract	Describes the service characteristics and supports service measurement tracking, governance, and audit.	Service Level
	Key Performance Indicator	Defines an objective that is measured, its requested threshold, and the calculation method to be used.	Service Level

Appendix E
IT4IT Foundation Certification Syllabus

UNIT 1	IT4IT Overview
Purpose	The purpose of this Learning Unit is to help the Candidate understand the IT4IT Reference Architecture at an overview level.
KLP Reference	1.*, 2.*, 3.*, 4.1
Learning Outcome	The Candidate must be able to: 1. Explain what The Open Group IT4IT Reference Architecture is and what approach it uses (KLP 1.2-1) 2. Identify the intended use of IT4IT Reference Architecture for organizations (KLP 4.1-1) 3. Identify the intended use of the IT4IT Reference Architecture for suppliers of IT management products and services (KLP 4.1-2) 4. List the guiding principles that the IT4IT framework adheres to (KLP 3.1-5) 5. Demonstrate understanding of the IT Value Chain (KLP 3.1-1) 6. Briefly describe the difference between the primary activities and supporting activities in the IT Value Chain (KLP 3.1-2) 7. List the primary activities of the IT Value Chain (KLP 3.1-3) 8. List the supporting activities of the IT Value Chain (KLP 3.1-4) 9. Explain the difference between value chain and value stream (KLP 3.2-2) 10. Briefly describe how the IT Value Chain supports the IT service lifecycle (KLP 3.3-1) 11. Briefly describe how the four value streams manage the full service lifecycle (KLP 3.3-2)
UNIT 2	**Definitions**
Purpose	The purpose of this Learning Unit is to help the Candidate understand the key terminology of the IT4IT Reference Architecture standard.
KLP Reference	2.*
Learning Outcome	The Candidate must be able to understand and explain the following definitions: 1. Service Lifecycle data object (data object) (KLP 2.1-1) 2. IT Value Chain (KLP 2.2-1) 3. Value chain (KLP 2.3-1)

	4. Value stream (KLP 2.4-1) 5. Functional component (KLP 2.5-1) 6. Service Model Backbone data object (KLP 2.6-1) 7. Relationship (KLP 2.7-1) 8. System of record (KLP 2.8-1) 9. IT service (KLP 2.9-1) It is expected that these definitions would be covered as part of the learning in other units.
UNIT 3	**Basic Concepts**
Purpose	The purpose of this Learning Unit is to help the Candidate understand the Basic Concepts of IT4IT value streams and the IT4IT Reference Architecture.
KLP Reference	3.*
Learning Outcome	The Candidate must be able to: 1. Briefly describe an overview of the Strategy to Portfolio (S2P) Value Stream (KLP 3.2-3) 2. Briefly describe an overview of the Requirement to Deploy (R2D) Value Stream (KLP 3.2-4) 3. Briefly describe an overview of the Request to Fulfill (R2F) Value Stream (KLP 3.2-5) 4. Briefly describe an overview of the Detect to Correct (D2C) Value Stream (KLP 3.2-6) 5. Describe what functional components and data objects are (KLP 3.2-7) 6. Explain the relationship of functional components to data objects (KLP 3.2-8) 7. Describe the scope of the S2P Value Stream (KLP 3.3-3) 8. List S2P value propositions (KLP 3.3-4) 9. List S2P typical activities (KLP 3.3-5) 10. Describe the scope of the R2D Value Stream (KLP 3.3-6) 11. List R2D value propositions (KLP 3.3-7) 12. List R2D typical activities (KLP 3.3-8) 13. Describe the scope of the R2F Value Stream (KLP 3.3-9) 14. List R2F value propositions (KLP 3.3-10) 15. List R2F typical activities (KLP 3.3-11) 16. Describe the scope of the D2C Value Stream (KLP 3.3-12) 17. List D2C value propositions (KLP 3.3-13) 18. List D2C typical activities (KLP 3.3-14) 19. Explain the concept of the four pillars "anchoring" the IT Value Chain – the Service Model, the Information Model, the Functional Model, and the Integration Model (KLP 3.4-1) 20. Explain the IT4IT Service Model (KLP 3.4-3) 21. Describe the Service Model Backbone (KLP 3.4-4) 22. Describe the IT4IT Information Model (KLP 3.4-5)

	23. State the characteristics of the service lifecycle data objects (KLP 3.4-6)
	24. Explain the difference between key and auxiliary data objects (KLP 3.4-8)
	25. State what the IT4IT Functional Model is (KLP 3.4-10)
	26. Explain functional components and how they relate to IT capability (KLP 3.4-11)
	27. Explain the difference between primary functional components and secondary functional components (KLP 3.4-12)
	28. Explain interactions between functional components and data objects (KLP 3.4-13)
	29. Explain what an IT service is (KLP 3.5-1)
UNIT 4	**IT4IT Core**
Purpose	The purpose of this Learning Unit is to help the Candidate understand the IT4IT Reference Architecture at a high level.
KLP Reference	4.*
Learning Outcome	The Candidate must be able to:
	1. List the five levels of IT4IT abstractions and identify which are vendor-agnostic and which are vendor-specific (KLP 4.2.1-1)
	2. Explain why an informal notation was chosen for Levels 1 and 2 (KLP 4.2.1-2)
	3. List the five core concepts introduced at Reference Architecture Level 1 (KLP 4.2.2-1)
	4. Explain the Level 1 class model (KLP 4.2.2-2)
	5. Explain the objective of the IT4IT Reference Architecture as it relates to Level 1 (KLP 4.2.2-3)
	6. Explain how the IT4IT Reference Architecture uses the value stream concept (KLP 4.2.2-4)
	7. List the three things a functional component must have (KLP 4.2.2-5)
	8. Identify the OMG definition that is aligned contextually with the service lifecycle data object (artifact) (KLP 4.2.2-6)
	9. Identify the constituent parts of the system of record fabric for IT management (KLP 4.2.2-7)
	10. Briefly explain the Level 1 Reference Architecture diagram (KLP 4.2.3-1)
	11. List the four additional concepts introduced at Reference Architecture Level 2 (KLP 4.2.4-1)
	12. Explain the Level 2 class model (KLP 4.2.4-2)
	13. Briefly explain an example Level 2 Reference Architecture diagram (KLP 4.2.5-1)
	14. Identify the primary method for communicating the IT4IT Reference Architecture specification at Level 3 (KLP 4.2.6-1)

	15. List the additional concepts introduced at Reference Architecture Level 3 (KLP 4.2.6-2) 16. Identify the notation used for the Level 3 Reference Architecture diagrams (KLP 4.2.7-1) 17. Explain who owns and controls Levels 4 and 5 of the Reference Architecture (KLP 4.2.8-1) 18. Explain what kind of content might be included in Level 4 (KLP 4.2.8-2) 19. Explain what kind of content might be included in Level 5 (KLP 4.2.8-3)
UNIT 5	**Strategy to Portfolio Value Stream**
Purpose	The purpose of this Learning Unit is to help the Candidate understand the objectives and functional components of the Strategy to Portfolio Value Stream.
KLP Reference	5.*
Learning Outcome	The Candidate must be able to: 1. Describe the objectives of the Strategy to Portfolio (S2P) Value Stream (KLP 5.1-1, KLP 5.1-2, KLP 5.1-3) 2. Explain the benefits of implementing the S2P Value Stream for the business (KLP 5.2-1) 3. List the KPIs (KLP 5.3-1) 4. Explain the purpose of the Enterprise Architecture functional component (KLP 5.4.1-1) 5. Briefly describe the key data object(s) associated with the Enterprise Architecture functional component (KLP 5.4.1-2) 6. Explain the purpose of the Policy functional component (KLP 5.4.2-1) 7. Briefly describe the key data object(s) associated with the Policy functional component (KLP 5.4.2-2) 8. Explain the purpose of the Proposal functional component (KLP 5.4.3-1) 9. Briefly describe the key data object(s) associated with the Proposal functional component (KLP 5.4.3-2) 10. Explain the purpose of the Portfolio Demand functional component (KLP 5.4.4-1) 11. Briefly describe the key data object(s) associated with the Portfolio Demand functional component (KLP 5.4.4-2) 12. Explain the purpose of the Service Portfolio functional component (KLP 5.4.5-1) 13. Briefly describe the key data object(s) associated with the Service Portfolio functional component (KLP 5.4.5-2) 14. Explain the purpose of the IT Investment Portfolio auxiliary functional component (KLP 5.4.6-1) 15. Briefly describe the key data object(s) associated with the IT Investment Portfolio auxiliary functional component (KLP 5.4.6-2)

UNIT 6	Requirement to Deploy Value Stream
Purpose	The purpose of this Learning Unit is to help the Candidate understand the objectives and functional components of the Requirement to Deploy Value Stream.
KLP Reference	6.*
Learning Outcome	The Candidate must be able to: 1. Describe the objectives of the Requirement to Deploy (R2D) Value Stream (KLP 6.1-1, KLP 6.1-2) 2. Explain the benefits of implementing the R2D Value Stream for the business (KLP 6.2-1) 3. List the KPIs (KLP 6.3-1) 4. Explain the purpose of the Project functional component (KLP 6.4.1-1) 5. Briefly describe the key data object(s) associated with the Project functional component (KLP 6.4.1-2) 6. Explain the purpose of the Requirement functional component (KLP 6.4.2-1) 7. Briefly describe the key data object(s) associated with the Requirement functional component (KLP 6.4.2-2) 8. Explain the purpose of the Service Design functional component (KLP 6.4.3-1) 9. Briefly describe the key data object(s) associated with the Service Design functional component (KLP 6.4.3-2) 10. Explain the purpose of the Source Control functional component (KLP 6.4.4-1) 11. Briefly describe the key data object(s) associated with the Source Control functional component (KLP 6.4.4-2) 12. Explain the purpose of the Build functional component (KLP 6.4.5-1) 13. Briefly describe the key data object(s) associated with the Build functional component (KLP 6.4.5-2) 14. Explain the purpose of the Build Package functional component (KLP 6.4.6-1) 15. Briefly describe the key data object(s) associated with the Build Package functional component (KLP 6.4.6-2) 16. Explain the purpose of the Release Composition functional component (KLP 6.4.7-1) 17. Briefly describe the key data object(s) associated with the Release Composition functional component (KLP 6.4.7-2) 18. Explain the purpose of the Test functional component (KLP 6.4.8-1) 19. Briefly describe the key data object(s) associated with the Test functional component (KLP 6.4.8-2) 20. Explain the purpose of the Defect functional component (KLP 6.4.9-1) 21. Briefly describe the key data object(s) associated with the Defect functional component (KLP 6.4.9-2)

UNIT 7	Request to Fulfill Value Stream
Purpose	The purpose of this Learning Unit is to help the Candidate understand the objectives and functional components of the Request to Fulfill Value Stream.
KLP Reference	7.*
Learning Outcome	The Candidate must be able to: 1. Describe the objectives of the Request to Fulfill (R2F) Value Stream (KLP 7.1-1, KLP 7.1-2, KLP 7.1-3) 2. Explain the benefits of implementing the R2F Value Stream for the business (KLP 7.2-1) 3. List the KPIs (KLP 7.3-1) 4. Explain the distinction between the purpose of primary and secondary functional components within the R2F Value Stream (KLP 7.4-1) 5. Explain the objectives of the Engagement Experience Portal (KLP 7.4-2) 6. Explain the purpose of the Engagement Experience Portal secondary functional component (KLP 7.4.1-1) 7. Briefly describe the key data object(s) associated with the Engagement Experience Portal secondary functional component (KLP 7.4.1-2) 8. Explain the purpose of the Offer Consumption functional component (KLP 7.4.4-1) 9. Briefly describe the key data object(s) associated with the Offer Consumption functional component (KLP 7.4.2-2) 10. Explain the purpose of the Offer Management functional component (KLP 7.4.3-1) 11. Briefly describe the key data object(s) associated with the Offer Management functional component (KLP 7.4.3-2) 12. Explain the purpose of the Catalog Composition functional component (KLP 7.4.4-1) 13. Briefly describe the key data object(s) associated with the Catalog Composition functional component (KLP 7.4.4-2) 14. Explain the purpose of the Request Rationalization functional component (KLP 7.4.5-1) 15. Briefly describe the key data object(s) associated with the Request Rationalization functional component (KLP 7.4.5-2) 16. Explain the purpose of the Fulfillment Execution functional component (KLP 7.4.6-1) 17. Briefly describe the key data object(s) associated with the Fulfillment Execution functional component (KLP 7.4.6-2) 18. Explain the purpose of the Usage functional component (KLP 7.4.7-1)

	19. Briefly describe the key data object(s) associated with the Usage functional component (KLP 7.4.7-2) 20. Explain the purpose of the Chargeback/Showback functional component (KLP 7.4.8-1) 21. Briefly describe the key data object(s) associated with the Chargeback/Showback functional component (KLP 7.4.8-2) 22. Explain the purpose of the Knowledge & Collaboration supporting function (KLP 7.4.9-1) 23. Briefly describe the key data object(s) associated with the Knowledge & Collaboration supporting function (KLP 7.4.9-2)
UNIT 8	**Detect to Correct Value Stream**
Purpose	The purpose of this Learning Unit is to help the Candidate understand the objectives and functional components model of the Detect to Correct Value Stream.
KLP Reference	8.*
Learning Outcome	The Candidate must be able to: 1. Describe the objectives of the Detect to Correct (D2C) Value Stream (KLP 8.1-1, KLP 8.1-2) 2. Explain the benefits of implementing the D2C Value Stream for the business (KLP 8.2-1) 3. List the KPIs (KLP 8.3-1) 4. (Not in use) 5. Explain the purpose of the Service Monitoring functional component (KLP 8.4.1-1) 6. Briefly describe the key data object(s) associated with the Service Monitoring functional component (KLP 8.4.1-2) 7. Explain the purpose of the Event functional component (KLP 8.4.2-1) 8. Briefly describe the key data object(s) associated with the Event functional component (KLP 8.4.2-2) 9. Explain the purpose of the Incident functional component (KLP 8.4.3-1) 10. Briefly describe the key data object(s) associated with the Incident functional component (KLP 8.4.3-2) 11. Explain the purpose of the Problem functional component (KLP 8.4.4-1) 12. Briefly describe the key data object(s) associated with the Problem functional component (KLP 8.4.4-2) 13. Explain the purpose of the Change Control functional component (KLP 8.4.5-1) 14. Briefly describe the key data object(s) associated with the Change Control functional component (KLP 8.4.5-2)

| | 15. Explain the purpose of the Configuration Management functional component (KLP 8.4.6-1)
16. Briefly describe the key data object(s) associated with the Configuration Management functional component (KLP 8.4.6-2)
17. Explain the purpose of the Diagnostics & Remediation functional component (KLP 8.4.7-1)
18. Briefly describe the key data object(s) associated with the Diagnostics & Remediation functional component (KLP 8.4.7-2)
19. Explain the purpose of the Service Level functional component (KLP 8.4.8-1)
20. Briefly describe the key data object(s) associated with the Service Level functional component (KLP 8.4.8-2)
21. List other IT operations capabilities that are not part of the D2C Value Stream (KLP 8.4.9-1) |
|---|---|
| **UNIT 9** | **IT4IT Certification Program** |
| **Purpose** | The purpose of this Learning Unit is to help the Candidate understand the IT4IT Certification Program. |
| **KLP Reference** | None. |
| **Learning Outcome** | The Candidate must be able to:
1. Explain the IT4IT Certification Program, and distinguish between the levels of certification. |

Acronyms and Abbreviations

API	Application Program Interface
BYOD	Bring Your Own Device
CapEx	Capital Expenditure
CI	Configuration Item
CMDB	Configuration Management Database
COBIT	Control Objectives for Information and Related Technology
DevOps	Development and Operations
DML	Definitive Media Library
eTOM	Business Process Framework (TM Forum)
IaaS	Infrastructure as a Service
ISACA	Information Systems Audit and Control Association
IT	Information Technology
ITIL	Information Technology Infrastructure Library
KPI	Key Performance Indicator
MTBF	Mean Time Between Failures
MTTR	Mean Time To Repair
OLA	Operational-Level Agreement
OMG	Object Management Group
OpEx	Operating Expenditure
PaaS	Platform as a Service
PMO	Project Management Office
RFC	Request for Change
SaaS	Software as a Service
SIEM	Security Information and Event Management
SLA	Service-Level Agreement
SLM	Service-Level Management
SLO	Service-Level Objective
TCO	Total Cost of Ownership
TMLA	Trademark License Agreement
UAT	User Acceptance Testing
UML	Unified Modeling Language

Index

A
abstraction
  Level 2 55, 56
  Level 3 56, 140
  levels 47
  Levels 4 and 5 58, 129
Agile 29
ArchiMate language 56, 140
auxiliary data object 39, 53
auxiliary functional component 15

B
Build data object 85
Build functional component 84
Build Package data object 85
Build Package functional component 85

C
capability 40
Catalog Composition functional component 101
certification principles 2
Change Control functional component 116
COBIT 42
Conversation data object 104

D
data object 38
Defect data object 88
Defect functional component 87
Detect to Correct 34, 126
Diagnostics & Remediation functional component 117

E
Engagement Experience Portal 98
Enterprise Architecture functional component 69
eTOM 42
Event data object 114
Event functional component 114

F
Fulfillment Execution functional component 102
Fulfillment Request data object 103
functional component 15, 40, 51, 124

I
IaaS 32
Incident data object 115
Incident functional component 114
Interaction data object 115
IT4IT Reference Architecture 36
ITIL 42
IT Initiative data object 82
IT Investment Portfolio auxiliary functional component 72
IT service lifecycle X, 14
IT Value Chain 13, 14, 138

K
key data object 39
Key Performance Indicator data object 118
Knowledge & Collaboration supporting function 104
Knowledge data object 104

O

Offer Catalog data object 100
Offer Consumption functional
   component 99
Offer data object 100
Offer Management functional
   component 100

P

PaaS 32
Physical Service Model 30
Policy data object 70
Policy functional component 70
Portfolio Backlog Item data object 71
Portfolio Demand functional component 71
primary activities 13, 123
primary functional component 41, 127
Problem functional component 115
Problem, Known Error data object 116
Project functional component 81
Proposal functional component 70

R

relationships 52
Release Composition functional
   component 86
Request data object 102
Request Rationalization functional
   component 101
Request to Fulfill 32, 95, 126
Requirement data object 82
Requirement functional component 82
Requirement to Deploy 29, 77, 125
RFC data object 116
Run Book data object 117

S

SaaS 32
SCRUM 29
secondary functional component 41, 127
Service Contract data object 118
Service Design functional component 82
Service Level functional component 118

service lifecycle data object 52
Service Model 34
Service Model Backbone 37, 126
Service Monitor data object 114
Service Monitoring functional
   component 113
Service Portfolio functional component 71
Shopping Cart data object 99
Source Control functional component 84
Source data object 84
Strategy to Portfolio 27, 65, 125
Subscription data object 102
supporting activities 13, 14, 123
system of record integration 53

T

Test Case data object 87
Test functional component 87

U

UML 56, 140
Usage data object 103
User Profile data object 99

V

value stream 14